MILLENNIUM
9

First published in 2002
jointly by

Gracewing
2 Southern Avenue
Leominster
Herefordshire HR6 0QF

Nova Millennium Romae
1 Largo Angelicum
00184 Roma
Italy

ISBN 0-85244-351-X

Printed by Rotostampa S.r.l.
Via Tiberio Imperatore, 23 - 00145 Roma

Antonio Cassanelli

Secretary of the "Giulio Ricci"
Diocesan Sindological Centre,
Rome

THE HOLY SHROUD

A comparison between the Gospel
narrative of the five stages of the Passion
(Flagellation, Crowning with Thorns,
Way of the Cross, Crucifixion and Burial),
and the Shroud as Evidence.

Translated by
Brian Williams

Contents

Preface

The Holy Father prays before the Shroud in the cathedral of Turin

The Shroud whispers: believe in God's love and flee from the misfortune of sin.

On the weekend of 23-24 May 2000, the Holy Father made a Pastoral Visit to Vercelli and Turin (Italy). The culmination of his pilgrimage was a visit on Sunday afternoon to the Holy Shroud, preserved in the Cathedral of Turin. There the Pope knelt in prayer before the Blessed Sacrament, and before the Shroud, and then presided at a brief Liturgy of the Word. After the reading of the Gospel (John 20: 3-8), the Holy Father gave the following address:

Dear Brothers and Sisters,

1. With my gaze turned to the Shroud, I would like to extend a cordial greeting to you all, the faithful of the Church of Turin. I greet the pilgrims who have come from every part of the world at the time of this public exposition, to look at one of the most unsettling signs of the Redeemeer's suffering love.

As I entered the Cathedral, which still shows the scars of last year's terrible fire, I paused in adoration before the Eucharist, the sacrament which is the focus of the Church's attention and, under humble appearances, contains the true, real and substantial presence of Christ. In the light of Christ's presence in our midst, I then stopped before the Shroud, the precious Linen that can help us better to understand the mystery of the love of God's son for us.

Before the Shroud, the intense and agonizing image of an unspeakable torment, I wish to thank the Lord for this unique gift, which asks for the believer's loving attention and complete willingness to follow the Lord.

2. The Shroud is a challenge to our intellligence. It first of all requires of every person, particularly the researcher, that he humbly grasp the profound message it sends to his reason and his life. The mysterious fascination of the Shroud forces questions to be raised about the sacred Linen and the historical life of Jesus. Since it is not a matter of faith, the Church has no specific competence to pronounce on these questions. She entrusts to scientists the task of continuing to investigate, so that satisfactory answers my be found to the questions connected with this Sheet which, according to tradition, wrapped the body of our Redeemer after he had been taken down from the Cross. The Church urges that the Shroud be studied without pre-established positions that take for granted results that are not such; she invites them to act with interior freedom and attentive respect for both scientific methodology and the sensibilities of believers.

3. For the believer, what counts above all is that the Shroud is a mirror of the Gospel. In fact if we reflect on the sacred Linen, we cannot escape the idea that the image it presents has such a profound relationship with what the Gospels tell us of Jesus' passion and death, that every sensitive person feels inwardly touched and moved at beholding it. Whoever approaches it is also aware that the Shroud does not hold people's hearts to itself, but turns them to him, at whose service the Father's loving providence has put it. Therefore it is right to foster an awareness of the precious value of this image, which everyone sees and no one at present can explain. For every

thoughtful person it is a reason for deep reflection, which can even involve one's life.

The Shroud is thus a truly unique sign that points to Jesus, the true Word of the Father, and invites us to pattern our lives on the life of the One who gave himself for us.

4. The image of human suffering is reflected in the Shroud. It reminds modern man, often distracted by prosperity and technological achievements, of the tragic situation of his many brothers and sisters, and invites him to question himself about the mystery of suffering in order to explain its causes. The imprint left by the tortured body of the Crucified One, which attests to the tremendous human capacity for causing pain and death to one's fellow men, stands as an icon of the suffering of the innocent in every age: of the countless tragedies that have marked past times and the dramas which continue to unfold in the world.

Before the Shroud, how can we not think of the millions of people who die of hunger, of the horrors committed in the many wars that soak nations in blood, of the brutal exploitation of women and children, of the millions of human beings who live in hardship and humiliation on the edges of great cities, especially in developing countries? How can we not recall with dismay and pity those who do not enjoy basic civil rights, the victims of torture and terrorism, the slaves of criminal organisations?

By calling to mind these tragic situations, the Shroud not only spurs us to abandon our selfishness, but leads us to discover the mystery of suffering, which, sanctified by Christ's sacrifice, achieves salvation for all humanity.

5. The Shroud is also an image of God's love as well as of human sin. It invites us to rediscover the ultimate reason for Jesus' redeeming death. In the incomparable suffering that it documents, the love of the One who "so loved the world that he gave his only son" (John 3:16) is made almost tangible and reveals its astonishing dimensions. In its presence believers can only exclaim in all truth: "Lord, you could not love me more!", and

immediately realise that sin is responsible for that suffering: the sins of every human being.

As it speaks to us of love and sin, the Shroud invites us all to impress upon our spirit the face of God's love, to remove from it the tremendous reality of sin. Contemplation of that tortured body helps contemporary man to free himself from the superficiality of the selfishness with which he frequently treats love and sin. Echoing the word of God and centuries of Christian consciousness, the Shroud whispers: believe in God's love, the greatest treasure given to humanity, and flee from sin, the greatest misfortune in history.

6. The Shroud is also an image of powerlessness: the powerlessness of death, in which the ultimate consequence of the mystery of the Incarnation is revealed. The burial cloth spurs us to measure ourselves against the most troubling aspect of the mystery of the Incarnation, which is also one that shows with how much truth God truly became man, taking on our condition in all things, except sin. Everyone is shaken by the thought that not even the Son of God withstood the power of death, but we are all moved at the thought that he so shared our human condition as willingly to subject himself to the total powerlessness of the moment when life is spent. It is the experience of Holy Saturday, an important stage on Jesus' path to Glory, from which a ray of light shines on the sorrow and death of every person. By reminding us of Christ's victory, faith gives us the certainty that the grave is not the ultimate goal of existence. God calls us to resurrection and immortal life.

7. The Shroud is an image of silence. There is a tragic silence of incommunicability, which finds its greatest expression in death, and there is the silence of fruitfulness, which belongs to whoever refrains from being heard outwardly in order to delve to the roots of truth and life. The Shroud expresses not only the silence of death but also the courageous and fruitful silence of triumph over the transitory, through total immersion in God's eternal present. It thus offers a moving confirmation of the fact that the merciful omnipotence of our God is not restrained by any power of evil, but

knows instead how to make the very power of evil contribute to good. Our age needs to rediscover the fruitfulness of silence, in order to overcome the dissipation of sounds, images and chatter that too often prevent the voice of God from being heard.

8. Dear brothers and sisters: your Archbishop, dear Cardinal Giovanni Saldarini, the Pontifical Guardian of the Holy Shroud, has offered the following words as the motto of this Solemn Exposition: "All will see your salvation". Yes, the pilgrimage that great throngs are making to this city is precisely a "coming to see" this tragic and enlightening sign of the Passion, which proclaims the Redeemer's love. This icon of Christ abandoned in the dramatic and solemn state of death, which for centuries has been the subject of significant representations, and for 100 years, thanks to photography, has been so frequently reproduced, urges us to go to the heart of the mystery of life and death, to discover the great and consoling message it haas left us. The Shroud shows us Jesus at the moment of his greatest helplessness and reminds us that in the abasement of that death lies the salvation of the whole world. The Shroud thus becomes an invitation to face every experience, including that of suffering and extreme helplessness, with the attitude of those who believe that God's merciful love overcomes every poverty, every limitation, every temptation to despair.

May the Spirit of God, who dwells in our hearts, instil in everyone the desire and generosity necessary for accepting the Shroud's message, and for making it the decisive inspiration of our lives.

In the Cathedral of Turin, jealously guarded there for over five centuries by the House of Savoy, is a venerated shroud whose fame has reached every part of the world, arousing the interest of historians, physicists, archæologists and theologians.

It is a burial-sheet in fine linen, similar to others which have come down to us from the ancient world, but unique because of the presence of stains, the origin, nature and intensity of which varies a good deal.

On the shroud, in a colour between carmine and mauve, there appears the faint image of a man who died after long and indescribable suffering.

If we study this body with great care, and we contemplate the incomparable face, if we compare the marks, the wounds and the signs of blows with the account contained in the Gospels, we are struck with amazement.

Everything coincides: we have valid motives for stating that this could indeed be the Holy Shroud, and on it, both suffering and glorious, the image of Christ the Redeemer.

The Shroud is one of the incalculable number of God's gifts, the kerygma (proclamation) of our salvation: "the wonderful document of His Passion, Death and Resurrection, written for us in letters of blood" (Paul VI in a dialogue with Monsignor G.Ricci).

SOME HISTORICAL NOTES

Ancient testimonies bear witness to the presence and veneration of a "Sacred Shroud" or "Sacred Face" from the first centuries of Christianity, in the middle eastern area, in Jerusalem, Edessa and Constantinople.

What we know as the Shroud of Turin appears for the first time in certain documentary history, around 1352, when it reached Lirey, along with the noble knight Geoffroi de Charny, Counsellor of the King and Standard Bearer of France.

In 1453 Marguerite de Charny, the last descendant of the family, gave custody of the Shroud to Anna di Lusignano, the wife of Duke Lodovico of Savoy, who transferred it to Chambéry, then Capital of Savoy.

Here, in the "Sainte Chapelle" during the night of 4 December 1532, the Shroud suffered very severe damage as a result of a fierce fire; the damage caused, even though lovingly repaired by the Poor Clares, is still evident.

In 1578, in order to ease the exhausting pilgrimage for St Charles Borromeo, who was travelling on foot and fasting to Chambéry, Duke Emanuel Philibert moved the Shroud to Turin, his new capital.

Since 1694, the Shroud has been preserved in the Chapel of the same name built between the Cathedral and the Royal Palace, to a design by the Theatine father and architect, Guarino Guarini.

Venerated beneath the famous dome, it is contained in an ornate urn, the three keys to which are separately in the possession of the Custodian, the Archbishop, and the Proprietor. The latter, by virtue of the will of Umberto (Humbert) of Savoy, the last king of Italy, is now, since 1983, the Holy Father himself.

The Shroud, stretched and stitched on to a backing of Holland canvas, has been preserved rolled up for its entire length around a wooden cylinder.

Only on occasions associated with the Church or the history of the House of Savoy was the Shroud exposed for the viewing of the faithful.

The relic has thus never left Turin, a city with which it has such deep associations, except that in 1706, during the siege by the French, it was taken for safe-keeping to Genoa, while in the terrible years of the Second World War, after a stay in the Quirinale, it was hidden in the Benedictine Monastery of Montevergine (Avellino).

In 1993, the restoration of the Chapel of the Shroud caused the relic to be provisionally transferred to the Choir of the Cathedral.

But the recent fearful fire which raged during the night of

11-12 April 1997, threatening the very existence of the Shroud from close quarters, raised in dramatic fashion the primary need for its protection and conservation.

For this purpose, a more suitable setting has been designed. An international commission for the purpose, aleady at work for some years, has drawn up a project which provides for the preservation of the Shroud "in a stretched-out position, flat and horizontal, in a casing of steel and bullet-proof glass, in a sterile condition free of air, and in the presence of inert gases. Protected from the light and maintained in constant and controlled climatic conditions".

With this careful scheme, the Shroud will be passed on to future generations and exposed for the vision of the pilgrims, who in greater and greater numbers come to contemplate this "document of the love of Christ", and "*to taste and see the gracious mercy of the Lord*" (Cardinal Giovanni Saldarini).

THE SCIENTIFIC STUDY OF THE SHROUD

The Shroud is in the form of a cloth strip, yellowish-white in colour, 4.37 metres long, 1.11 metres wide and 1.450 Kg in weight. It shows, close to each other at the head, the front and rear imprint of the body of a man.

From the archæological standpoint, the Shroud is a burial-sheet, wrapped round a corpse on the table in the tomb where the body was laid. To forensic medical examination, the image of the body seems to be stiffened by rigor mortis, and reveals a whole series of wounds and injuries corresponding to those recounted in the Gospels as being inflicted on Jesus. Signs of flagellation over the whole body, small wounds in the scalp caused by a helmet of thorns, two torn areas in the left scapula zone and the right super-scapular zone, holes in the wrists and at the feet, which could be caused by the penetration of nails, and a wide injury caused by a steel weapon in the lower right rib region.

A thousand-year-old tradition has recognized this Shroud as the burial-sheet of Christ, and today science states that this is an admissable claim.

The study of the Shroud began in 1898, when on the occasion of a public viewing granted for the fourth centenary of the consecration of the Cathedral, the fiftieth anniversary of the Statute granted by Charles Albert, and the wedding of Crown Prince Victor Emanuel of Savoy and Helena of Montenegro, King Humbert I allowed the lawyer from Asti, Secondo Pia, to take the first photographs.

"Shut away in my dark room, and absorbed in my work, I felt a surge of very strong emotion when, during the development of the prints, I saw the Holy Face appear for the first time on the plate, with such clarity that I was dumbfounded" (Memoir of Secondo Pia).

The photographic technique gave a negative view of the image on the shroud; in other words, the imprint of the body is positive on the photographic negative, while it remains negative on the original and the photographic offprints. This, however, is not true of the stains, which have always been assumed to be bloodstains, and thus appear positive on the material.

In 1969, Humbert II of Savoy, and Cardinal Michele Pellegrino, then Archbishop of Turin, named a commission of experts of the highest level, and thus laid the basis for a rational scientific examination, with the use of avant-garde techniques and methods.

In this way, thanks above all to the Commission, excellent results were to be obtained both at the International Sindonological Centre in Turin and at the American Commission of STURP (Shroud of Turin Research Project, 1977).

Today, after thirty years, we are able to establish that:

— the Shroud was hand-woven, and conforms to the normal usage in the middle east of 2000 years ago;

— the presence of aloes and myrrh is discernible on the material;

— among the fibres have been found and identified pollen from plants, which confirms the journeys of the Shroud from Palestine, across Anatolia, and into Europe;

— three-dimensional photographs confirm the volumetric presence of an object lying under the sheet;

— the image is not due to paint pigments and there are no artist's brush-strokes;

— human blood of the AB group is present from veins and arteries, both during life and after death.

— the sheet has contained the body of a dead man;

— it is possible to recover fragments of DNA.

These are extremely interesting and important discoveries, irrefutable data capable of combatting many of the inherent doubts about the authenticity of the Shroud. But while the calm conviction grows in us, we nevertheless have a strict duty to be extremely prudent until definitive conclusions can be reached.

The controversial result of the analysis for dating by radio-carbon tests has in fact held up since 1988 a programme of research which aimed at a series of investigations in the various analytical contexts, of which that effected by using C14 was only one element taken out of context.

As is well-known, the analysis, entrusted to the laboratories of Oxford, Tucson and Zurich, under the coordination of the British Museum in London, provided a dating between 1260 and 1390 in the Christian era.

Monsignor Ricci had not accepted the findings, and gave his reasons, and the latest theories on the matter seem in fact to have justified him. While the authoritative nature of the laboratories in question must exclude any irregularities in the techniques and methods used, it is very likely that they came to those conclusions because during the conduct of their work they did not take account of the alterations suffered by the material as a result of fires and pollution over the course of the centuries.

It is to be hoped that the scientists will coordinate their findings and resume their studies with calm and professional skill.

Monsignor Ricci wrote: «*Men of faith wish for the scientific research; they demand that it should be done with seriousness and they deem it necessary not for faith itself but for those "preambles" of which St Thomas speaks when he states that "true science demonstrates the presuppositions of faith"*».

THE IMAGE OF THE SHROUD IN ART

The Council in the Trullo in 691 (a derivation from the third Council of Constantinople in the 680s) ordered that "*the figure of Christ our God be exalted and also painted in images, under human form, instead of the ancient Lamb*". This was the culmination of centuries of struggle against the Christological heresies, and marked a strengthening in the doctrinal knowledge of the clergy and laity, overcoming psychological blocks associated with forms of respect and fear of causing scandal.

The artists who undertook the work of representing the "Suffering Christ" therefore found themselves without previous models.

It is extraordinary how images of the Holy Face, from the sixth to the thirteenth centuries, in Byzantine iconography, beginning in Constantinople and radiating out towards the Slavonic world and towards Italy (one example which can serve for all, the Pantocrator of the apse in Monreale - Sicily) resemble each other everywhere, and seem to have taken their initial inspiration from one single original: the Face of the Shroud.

It is from a mistaken reading of the Holy Shroud, in fact that the enormous eyes of the Byzantine Christ are derived, and the longer moustache on the right, and the wisp of hair on the forehead, to mention only a few of the most obvious characteristics.

And still today, by very ancient tradition, Greek and Slavic icons which portray the Face of Jesus, lovingly venerated in the "best corner of the house", are known as "Mandylion" (napkin), "Acheropoeta" (not made with hands) and "Apomaxis" (imprint), and all bear a strong resemblance to one another.

As we mentioned, in the absence of a previous model, and of precise historical sources on the crucifixion, the artists were forced to supply the gap by their own imaginations.

The history of art, from the sixth century to today, is rich in distinguished works centering on the saving sacrifice of the Son of God. As an expression of both genius and faith, they have led generations of the faithful who feel such a keen awareness of the need for an image, to prayer.

But the portrayal of Jesus bearing the cross entirely on his shoulders, or nailed to it with four nails passing through the palms of his hands and through both feet do not in fact correspond to the reality.

It is once again the Holy Shroud which comes to our aid in shedding light on our awareness of what truly happened in Holy Week.

AN INVITATION TO PRAYER

I believe that the best attitude with which the Christian can approach the Shroud is one of humility and prayer, for this is the way we can approach Jesus himself and his Passion through contemplation of it.

The Shroud invites us to pray: "*a constant, unceasing prayer which asks for nothing in particular because it asks everything; that prayer whose rhythm the mystics liken to breathing, to the very beating of the heart. It is the prayer which transfigures the world, the prayer which makes life a constant act of thanksgiving and faith, a constant plea for forgiveness because the world has a constant need to be pardoned*".

But prayer of this kind implies a faith lived out in everyday life, fed by the grace of the Sacraments. Only this way, in an unending dialogue with God, will the Holy Shroud unfold all its wounds to us, revealing itself in the splendour of the theological message.

"Thus we understand the profound value of the humiliation of the Word of God; we are induced to remember His earthly life, his divine passion and saving death, and the redemption which entered the world with him" (Article LXXXII of the Council in the Trullo).

Our faith is based on revealed truth and has its foundations in the Holy Scriptures, in the tradition of the Fathers, and in the teaching of the Church. In a special way, the Evangelists, illuminated by the Spirit of Truth, *"faithfully handed down to us what Jesus, the Son of God, during His life among men, did and taught for our eternal salvation"* (Dei Verbum, 19).

The Holy Shroud does not, therefore, add anything to the Good News, but it may satisfy our desire to know how Jesus had to suffer for us, and – if we are truly disposed towards it – may lead us to meditation and prayer.

Every drop of blood absorbed by the material, every mark still impressed on the weft of the linen, is an exceptional witness of the Gospel, capable of revealing to us situations, proceedings and events which would otherwise have remained unknown. By using the discoveries of archaeology, of forensic science and physics, it has been possible to establish the genuineness of the Shroud, and work is still going on to declare its authenticity.

Whatever the conclusions of the research may be, the Holy Shroud is and always will remain the incomparable icon of the Risen Lord: "icon" understood not as an art object but as a theological discourse, a sacramental presence, a vehicle of the transmission of sanctifying Grace, as it is understood in the Eastern Church.

Through the Shroud we can relive the first Holy Week of history in Jerusalem. And we can see – like new disciples – Jesus climbing the hill to Calvary, offering His life for us, and dying on the Cross. We can, like Saints Peter and John, hurry to the sepulchre to see, and believe, and announce to the brethren "Christ is risen! Alleluia!".

IN THE FOOTSTEPS OF MONSIGNOR RICCI

The contemplation and study of the Shroud makes it possible for us to follow the Passion of Jesus through all its phases: flagellation, crowning with thorns, the way of the cross, the crucifixion and the burial.

In this quest, the "Apostle of the Shroud", Monsignor Giulio Ricci, succeeded in participating in a very special way. For more than fifty years, keeping in close contact with the most advanced research centres in the world, he himself studied the Shroud with ever-deepening and more exhaustive research. His tireless commitment and his enthusiasm led him to undertake a dialogue with the greatest experts on the Shroud, with famous theologians and biblical scholars, and to discuss the fruits of his studies with many bishops and cardinals. He personally suggested research and analysis to Humbert II of Savoy, and was finally received and listened to attentively by Pope Paul VI.

By comparing the theological, exegetical, archæological, clinical, juridical and sindonological aspects of the relic, Mgr. Ricci made some original discoveries. His studies in the field of bodily measurement, and the subsequent axonometric reconstructions were quite exceptional, as were those in the goniometric measurement of the blood trickles.

These studies, whose results were confirmed by Prof. Enrico Medi, the great scientist and theologian who holds the Chair of Physics at the University of Rome, permitted Mgr. Ricci to reconstruct the Passion of Jesus, to expound it in his books and represent it in pictorial and sculptural form at exhibitions, conferences and congresses all over the world.

Symbolic of this is his "Shroud-inspired Crucifix", designed and created on the basis of a deeply sensitive study of the Shroud, with a devotional precedent only in that painted by St. Alfonso Maria de' Liguori. In this image, art, science and faith mingle in the dramatic moment of the sacrifice of Jesus.

Now Monsignor Ricci, illuminated by the Lord, contemplates in heaven the Sacred Face of Jesus, so beloved by him on earth. Our commitment is to follow in his footsteps, and to continue on the path which he pointed out to us.

The Flagellation

The Sanhedrin, when it handed Jesus over to the judgment of Pilate, the Roman Procurator, certainly did not intend to pay homage to the foreign power. It was aiming to obtain the death sentence which it no longer had the right to inflict (since 63 B.C.).

Pilate was well aware of the innocence of Jesus, at least according to Roman Law, but since every excuse for setting him free proved vain, and he himself was torn between the certainty of the law and the expediency of politics, he decided to give satisfaction to the crowd, in an attempt to placate their angry insistence.

"I will subject him to a whipping, then release him" (Luke 23:16). Jesus is thus condemned to the terrible punishment of flagellation. For the Jews, the use of flagellation was regulated by the Book of Deuteronomy, and the number of blows, proportionate to the seriousness of the crime, must never exceed forty minus one. The "Cives Romani", thanks to the "lex Porcia a tergo civium" of 195 B.C., were exonerated from this penalty, and could only be subjected to ordinary whipping or beating with rods after due process of law. However, the Romans used flagellation against subject peoples, slaves and Romans condemned to death.

This penalty, inflicted without any limitation of blows by torture instruments known as the flagellum, flagrum and scutica, was used:
— to force someone to reveal a secret;
— as a penalty for a minor crime;
— as an anticipation of capital punishment.

Flagellation was often inflicted by men trained in the "Gymnasium flagri", capable of striking or avoiding every part of the body of the condemned man with precision.

The rivulets of the coagulated blood of Jesus which were then to be transferred to the linen sheet, by heamolysis and fibrinolysis in the tomb, owing to the haemolithic action of the ointment and the emollient effect of the aloes and myrrh, tell us that:

Jeus was flagellated "according to Roman custom" – i.e. stripped and tied by the wrists to a low column (*). There were two men who delivered the blows, one to the right and one to the left of him. They inflicted their blows with geometric precision, avoiding the cardiac zone so as not to kill him.

In fact, according to Pilate's orders, the flagellation should be a punishment from which the victim should come out alive. Blows on the heart, in contrast, would have caused a traumatic serous pericarditis, with lethal consequences.

The body of Jesus was mercilessly tormented. On the Shroud 121 strokes can be counted. But if the torturers were using the "flagrum taxillatum", a whip fitted with three strands terminating in a double "taxillo" (small pellet) with a handle and two sharpened spheres, the bruising and flesh-rending blows were far, far more numerous.

"The plowers plowed upon my back; they have made long furrows thereon" (Psalm 129: 3).

(*) A similar column, 65 cm high, can be seen in Rome, in San Prassede all'Esquilino. Found by Cardinal Colonna in Jerusalem, it was brought to Rome by him in 1213.

The Crown of Thorns and the Sacred Visage

"And the soldiers plaited a crown of thorns and put it on his head" (John 19: 2).

The soldiers who assault Jesus are probably not Roman legionaries, but "auxiliaries" recruited from among the neighbouring populations, faithful to Rome, but fiercely hostile to the Jews.

On their own initiative they take their cue from the charge made against Jesus, and inveigh against him, mocking the "King of the Jews".

Hence the purple mantle, the reed as a sceptre, and the terrible crown. This, woven at the very least out of thorny twigs, is revealed as a helmet of intense suffering. «Και οι στρατιωται πλεξαντες στεφανον εξ ακανθων επεθηκαν αυτου τη κεφαλη». «Et milites, plectentes coronam de spinis, imposuerunt capiti Eius». The verb 'τιθημι' is illuminating for us; it has the prefix 'εμι' which has the precise meaning of placing upon – rather than around – 'περι' - the head. It is a shade of interpretation by which John implicitly describes the use not of the slender coronet of thorns imagined by the artists, but a *helmet* made of thorns. The whole top of the skull and the right and left of the forehead of the image on the shroud are marked with signs of blood. The blood is from veins and arteries, especially abundant at the neck and on the forehead, with the trickles forming an epsilon "ε". This "ε" on the forehead, coming from one of its veins and formed along the wrinkles marked by the strain and the spasms of pain, is characteristic.

In many of the paintings from the sixth to the eleventh centuries, Christ is represented with a quiff of hair at his forehead. The link with the face on the Shroud is clear, and it must have been known, at least approximately, in these centuries.

On the neck there are eight wounds, from which issue twelve rivulets of blood, seven on the left, three on the right and one vertical. The prevailing direction of the blood trickles towards the left stresses the unnatural position which was forced on Jesus as he suffered blows and insults.

Finally, we may suppose that Jesus, in contrast to the way in which he is represented in classical iconography, climbed up to Calvary and died on the cross without the crown of thorns.

The shroud, in harmony with the Gospels, tells us that Jesus, laden with the *patibulum* on his shoulders, went on the Via Crucis wearing his seamless robe. In order to put it on, they had necessarily to take off the Crown of thorns which had been placed on his head.

We do not have any evidence either to state that the crown was newly placed on Jesus' head along the *deductio*, to be taken off again on Golgotha and replaced on his head when, stripped of his garments, he was nailed to the Cross.

The seamless tunic, with the opening at the neck, would not have been possible to take on or off without removing the crown.

These are only hypotheses, but I believe they are very close to the true facts.

The crown of thorns, present or not on the Cross itself, is in any case for us the tangible reminder of the sufferings of the Innocent One, who gave his life for us.

The Face of the Shroud has always inspired artists and the faithful.

For the Sacred Visage is *"divinely beautiful, and irradiates majesty and peace, but above all love and life. It also radiates an indefinable light, the goodness of which penetrates our hearts, a strength quite out of the common, which conquers us with its absolute greatness".*

"This face, so inimitable and real, is the summing up of all human faces ... the self-portrait of Christ and at the same time the portrait of humanity itself: "Behold the Man" – *sorrow and grandeur are his dimensions.*

"Christ who is lowly and humble of heart is not in haste; he approaches and reveals his true face almost without our realising it. For, as the Apostle Paul says, our way of seeing is imperfect, we see through a glass, darkly, through a veil...

"If, in contemplating the image of the Shroud, we wish to recognise the light of Christ which irradiates his tormented face, we must close our eyes and open our hearts" (Il Volto di Dio, il volto dell'uomo – Stano Dusik).

Each of us, when we stand before the Sacred Visage, can commit ourselves to undoing the wrongs suffered by Jesus; by prayer, and by a life-style based on the teachings of the Gospel.

Finally, let us make the prayer of Paul VI our own: "We ask of You, Lord, your Spirit of Love, of comprehension and sacrifice, to bring effective help to those whom we find suffering along the path of our life. Inspire us with the gestures which bring relief, the words which illuminate, the love which comforts...

"Help us to respond to the cry of those who suffer: It is your cry!".

The Condemnation

"Behold the Man" (John 19: 5).

Pilate, aware of the innocence of this extraordinary accused man, and struck by his words: *"I have come into the world to bear witness to the truth ... you would have no power over me if it had not been given to you from above"* (John 19: 11), tries again to save Jesus.

The crowd, confronted with this man lacerated by the whipping and crowned with thorns, should be moved with compassion and cease their demands.

But instead, the Jews stir up emotions and come near to a riot, crying "Crucify him, Crucify him!", and in order to convince the Roman Procurator finally, they cast doubts on his loyalty to Caesar.

At this point, Pilate, concerned by the behaviour of the crowd and fearful of negative repercussions on his career, gives in to them unconditionally.

He washes his hands, dissociating himself from the wishes of the Jews, but nevertheless he finally signs the order condemning Jesus to the Cross.

And although he had proclaimed *"I find no fault in him"* (John 18: 38), he delivers a regular death sentence. This sentence will have been transcribed in the archives of the Province and forwarded to Rome. The sentence has immediate effect.

Pilate also prepares the "titulus", bearing in Hebrew, Greek and Latin, the charge against the condemned man: "Jesus of Nazareth, King of the Jews".

The Way of the Cross and the Crucifixion

Crucifixion – *"that most cruel and dreadful punishment"*, as Cicero described it, caused horror to the Roman people. The Jewish world, although it reserved condemnation to stoning for the most serious and ignominious crimes, had encountered death by impaling during the Babylonian captivity, and, with the invasion by Pompey the Great in 69 B.C., they had also become acquainted with capital punishment by means of the cross.

In the first ten years of the Roman Empire, and thus in the time of Jesus, the cross was used for the most serious punishment. It was constructed either in the shape of a $+$ (immissus) or of a T (commissus), and very rarely as an X (decusatus); the height was not more than 2 metres.

At the time of the execution, the cross was prepared by fixing the vertical shaft or "stipes" in the ground and making the condemned prisoner carry the horizontal shaft or "patibulum", binding it to his shoulders. The carrying out of the procedure was entrusted to an armed squad, in charge of which was a centurion. As he was responsible for overseeing the execution, he had also to certify the death of the crucified victims at the end.

The cross-bearing condamned, preceded by a slave carrying the "titulus", and surrounded by soldiers who urged them on with blows of the whip, came from the prison to the place where they were to meet the sentence, following the most crowded route possible. The crowd participated, by making the condemned men the object of mockery and obscenity. The authorities allowed this to go unchecked, so that the condemnation would receive the highest public notice.

For Jesus, though a voluntary and innocent victim, the same things took place.

"Despised and rejected of men; a man of sorrows and acquainted with grief... Yet he hath taken our sufferings upon him, and is burdened with our sorrows" (Isaiah 53: 3-4).

"You shall stretch out your arm, and another will bind you, and lead you where you would not go" (John 21: 18).

Jesus, stripped of the royal robe and released from the crown of thorns, is reclothed in his own garments. This robe was to protect his shoulders along the road to Calvary. On his shoulders, and the length of his arm, the "patibulum" is imposed – a not very long beam of around 40 kg in weight. It is attached to him, from right to left, by a rope tied also to the other two condemned men, and bound to his left ankle.

The procession moves off, and Jesus is led away, like a lamb to the slaughter in the Temple on Mount Moira, to the sacrifice on Golgotha. The crowd yells, the soldiers whip the other two prisoners, who twist and turn.

Jesus, already sorely tried by the whipping and by a moral sorrow which tears at his heart, falls disastrously to the pavement, without being able to protect himself in any way. His face is swollen, the nose distorted and his resistance is at its lowest.

The Shroud shows us a face in which the eyebrow arches are swollen and bruised, the cartilage of the nose broken, the lower lip contused.

Jesus might have died along the route, and the centurion, in order to avoid this, took the unusual step of calling on a passer-by to help. Simon of Cyrene relieved Jesus' pain, and helped to carry His "cross".

This countryman, who was returning, quite unaware of what was happening, from the fields where he worked to his home, and found himself in his small way relieving an unbearable situation, seems to me to represent in a perfect way the figure of the friend sent by Providence at the moment of greatest need.

The procession moves on: among the hostile crowd there is one who is immensely close to him, and sharing in his sufferings: Mary. Their gazes meet in a dialogue of ineffable communion and love. The Word made Flesh looks on his mother with gratitude and love; she contemplates Her Son and "a sword pierces her heart" (Luke 2: 35).

From the *Sanhedrin* (43a) it is known that there was in Jerusalem a religious guild of women who, at executions, provided the offering of wine or drugs to alleviate the sufferings of the condemned. It is possible that these pious women were also present at the execution of Jesus. One of them, coming forward, may have wiped the face of Jesus with a cloth, and the Shroud confirms this, especially on the left hand side.

It is from this gesture of loving concern that the story of Veronica arose.

Finally, the procession reaches Golgotha, a small piece of raised ground just outside the walls of Jerusalem, beyond the Gate of Ephraim, near an abandoned stone quarry.

His clothes are removed – and the stripping reopens the wounds – and Jesus is pushed to the ground and his arms are pinioned, with carefully aimed blows, to the "patibulum", by means of nails through his hands. But the study of the Shroud, together with careful Laboratory tests, has shown that the nails, in contrast to the traditional description, did not pass through the palms of the hands. In fact these would not have sustained the weight of the body, and would have torn. The nails were actually hammered through the Destot space – a gap existing in the wrist, corresponding to the carpus.

The executioners, who were well acquainted with the technique of crucifixion, knew that by fixing the nails at that point, they were attaching the body to the cross right up to the moment of death.

The pain is overwhelming, because in this way the nail penetrates the sensory nerve, and forces the thumb to curl. And it is important to note that the Shroud's image has no sign of a thumb.

Jesus, nailed to the "patibulum" is raised up on the "stipes". The body is pushed upward, and the legs bent. They fix his feet, the left over the right, with a single nail in the second metatarsal space. The "rose of blood" present around the hole in the right foot, instead of trickles of blood, is obvious proof that the left foot was in direct contact, and placed over the other.

The Death on the Cross

Though he was divine in nature, he counted it not a prize to be on an equality with God, and emptied himself, taking the form of a servant, being made in the likeness of man; and being found in fashion as a man, he humbled himself, becoming obedient even unto death, yea, the death of the cross" (Philippian 2: 6-8).

We have now reached the culmination of the saving sacrifice of the Son of God. Jesus, who came into the world to proclaim the immense love of the Father, was not understood, and in the most dramatic of all revelations, he offers the gift of himself.

Jesus is on the Cross: he is suffering and can scarcely breathe, and yet his words are still words of love. He forgives those who have condemned him, and promises Paradise to those who call on him (Luke 23: 34-43).

To avoid asphyxia, he raises himself, straining at the nail in his feet, but the effort is overwhelming.

Then Jesus turns his gaze towards the "Sorrowing Mother", and towards his beloved disciple, John, the only one of the twelve to be present. With infinite love he commends them to one another. And at the same time he commends the whole of humanity to his Mother.

Mary, the Mother of Christ, becomes our "Merciful mother, mediatrix of grace, luminous gateway leading us to heaven".

The hours pass. Jesus lowers and raises himself several times, then the muscular tension finally transfixes him in the suspended position. He is in his last agony, but he is not alone. With him, in him, respecting his humanity to the very limits of its freedom, is God the Father, is God the Holy Spirit of consolation, who will soon illuminate the hearts of humankind.

He cries *"My God, my God, why didst thou forsake me?"* (Matthew 27: 46), and this is not a lament, but the proclamation, the awareness that this Psalm 121 in its entirety refers to him.

Finally, after having asked for something to drink, he exclaims "*Father, into Thy hands I commend my spirit*" (Luke 23: 46) then "*giving a great cry*" (Mark 15: 37) and "*bowing his head, he yielded up his spirit*" (John 19: 31).

The Holy Shroud, united to what we are told in the Gospels, allows us invaluable insight into the movements of Jesus on the cross.

The laceration and bruising of the left metacarpal crown, caused by the rotary movement of the forearm around the nail, and by the friction against the wood of the cross, confirms that Jesus alternated between collapse and raising himself up. Only by raising himself up, in fact, could he have been able to breathe, to speak and to utter a cry.

The determining element is the study of the direction of the blood-flow along the forearms: the diamond-shaped path and the gathering in a clot at the right elbow (the body, when it raised itself upwards, moved to the right, making the right forearm adopt an almost vertical position). The goniometric measurement at the left carpus shows an angle of 35° between one trickle of blood and the other.

Many hypotheses have been formed about the physical cause of Jesus' death. Asphyxia, traumatic shock and serous pericarditis have all been cited. But these diagnoses, apart from any scientific critical study, all fail when confronted with the Gospel. For these accounts presuppose that Jesus died in a state of unconsciousness, and this is in sharp contrast to the whole theology of the Passion.

If we listen instead to the account of John, whose priceless testimony is that of an *eye witness*:

"*It was the day of the Preparation, and the Jews, so that the bodies should not remain upon the cross (for that Sabbath was a high festival), asked of Pilate that their legs should be broken and they should be taken away. The soldiers therefore came and broke the legs of the first and then of the other that had been crucified with him. But when they came to Jesus, and saw that he was dead already, they did not break his legs, but one of the soldiers pierced his side with a spear, and immediately bood and water issued out"* (John 19: 31-34).

This fact of water and blood pouring out at once tells us much. Jesus may have died of haemopericardium. The English medical expert William Stroud had already put forward this theory as far back as 1847. When carrying out an autopsy on persons who had died of haemopericardium, Dr Stroud had noted that in fact, when the pericardium is opened, the blood is revealed to be divided into two elements: plasma (transparent, like water) sedimented above, and the heavier corpusculated element deposited below. This was the reason why "blood and water immediately issued forth" from Jesus' side.

The hypothesis that the cause of death is to be attributed to the breaking or puncturing of the heart of Jesus would be attributable to an acute ischaemia of the heart.

The process of heart failure would have begun in the olive garden: *"And as he was in agony, he prayed even more intensely and his sweat became as it were drops of blood falling to the ground"* (Luke 22: 44), and it ended on the cross.

The modern chronology of Holy Week places the agony in Gethsemane on Tuesday evening, three days before the crucifixion. Three days of atrocious suffering, both physical and mental, capable of leading a heart already sorely tried to its destruction by failure followed by haemopericardium.

The Burial

The sun was beginning to set, and at the feet of Jesus, after the spectators had gone away to prepare for the coming feast, St John, Mary the Mother of Jesus and some reverent women remained alone.

The body of Jesus, according to Jewish law, would soon be taken away and thrown into the common ditch. If an honoured burial were to be assured, there was a need for immediate action, with determination, making the application in the right way and to the right person.

But Jesus seemed no longer to have friends or disciples: St John was too young and too inexpert, and Mary, as a woman, carried no weight before the law of those times. Thus it was that Joseph of Arimathaea, *"a member of the Sanhedrin, and a just man"* (Luke 23: 50), perhaps at the plea of Mary, risked the criticism of the Sanhedrin and *"boldly"* (Mark 15: 43) went to Pilate.

Roman law in fact ruled that *"corpora animadversorum quibuslibet petentibus ad sepulturam danda sunto"* (Dig. XLVIII, 24, no. 3) (the bodies of those punished are to be given to any who shall petition for their burial), and again that *"corpora ... cognatis eorum neganda non sunt"* (the bodies are not to be denied to their relations).

The body of the condemned, which belonged to the Procurator, was handed over for reverend burial to anyone who requested it, and especially to relatives. Pilate, in recognition of the authoritative position of Joseph of Arimathaea, and of the assurance that a new tomb would be used for the burial (as required by the Jewish Law, see Sanh. 7.b), when he had demanded and obtained the confirmation from the Centurion that Jesus was dead, issued the written authorisation (Mark 15: 42-45).

Joseph of Arimathæa, carrying in his hand the authorisation from the Procurator, moved rapidly through Jerusalem, as the city prepared for the feast. Probably he barely had time to call into a shop and buy a shroud. He chose the best, without quibbling over size or price, and headed quickly towards Calvary.

The trumpets of the Temple sounded for the second time. This call, from the top of the portico, announced the Sabbath. At the sound of the first call, work in the fields ceased, and at the second, the workshops and stalls closed, at the third all the pots were removed from the kiln, and the lamps were lit as the doors of the city closed.

The shrill notes of the trumpet marked the apparition of the first three stars in the sky. At the first star, it was vesper-time; at the second, between one day and the next, and at the third the new day dawned. In Jerusalem on that fourteenth Nisan of the year 785 "from the foundation of the city of Rome" (according to the calculations of the Bremen Observatory) the sun set at 18.08 while the appearance of the third star would have been around 19.08. And since Mark tells us that Joseph of Arimathæa acted "when even was come", he must have taken at least a half hour between obtaining the authorisation from Pilate, purchasing the shroud and returning to Calvary.

After showing the permit to the soldiers, only thirty minutes remained for the procedure for Jesus' burial. According to the complicated Jewish ritual, this was impossible. Thus, the choice had to fall on a temporary tomb, which was permitted by law.

Once the festival was over, the final burial according to the rites would be carried out: the seven washings of the body, the cutting of the hair and the nails, the anointing with perfumes, and the vesting with the "tachrichin" or burial robe. All this must be done without contact between the sexes. The men would carry out all the operations, while the women would collaborate by bringing and preparing the perfumes outside the Tomb.

Jesus is taken down lovingly from the cross. The nail is extracted from his feet, the patibulum is separated from the stipes, so that the revered body falls forward, and then finally the nails are extracted from his wrists. The blood remaining in the lower region of Jesus' body because of bodily hypostasis, flows out from the wound in his right side when the body is placed on the ground. The Holy Shroud clearly shows in the area of the kidneys the rivulet of post-mortal blood.

Blood also flows out from the wounds in the feet, once the nail has been removed. The close, detailed and prayerful study by Mons. Ricci has made it possible even to discern the fingerprints of those who raised Jesus' body up for its passage to the tomb. He has discovered and pointed out the imprint of the little finger, and ring and middle fingers of the left hand of whoever lifted Jesus' left foot, and was soaked in the blood that issued from the nail wound.

The sad procession moves silently towards the new tomb offered by Joseph of Arimathæa. It is only a few yards, 23 metres in all, but during the short journey the sacred Face is covered, out of love and respect, by a small cloth. As this absorbs in great measure the blood and sweat present on the face of Jesus, it will make it possible for the Shroud to portray a Face that was quite clean, and defined in its lineaments.

According to tradition, this cloth corresponds to the Sudario of Oviedo, and has been venerated in the capital of the Asturias since at least the ninth century.

The cloth, which measures 83 cm long and 52.5 cm wide, shows no image, but only stains.

Careful studies have ascertained the presence of human blood of Group AB, and the coincidence of the imprint, duplicated and specular, with the Face on the Shroud.

Relevant is the contribution by Monsignor Ricci who went to Oviedo the first time in 1965.

In the meantime, Nicodemus also arrived, carrying a mixture of myrrh and aloes, weighing about one hundred pounds (John 19: 39). After entering the tomb, St John, Joseph of Arimathæa, Nicodemus, and almost certainly Jesus' Mother, carefully laid the body of Jesus on the sepulchral shelf where the shroud had already been spread out. Strewn with aloes and myrrh, and other resinous oils, this is folded over the body of Jesus from head to foot, wrapped around the sides, and bound close to the body with several strips.

But time was now running out: after a final careful check, his most faithful followers must leave him. They come out of the tomb, and heave a great stone in front of it, then return in haste to Jerusalem.

"And the sabbath began to draw on" (Luke 23: 54).

Thanks to Mary

If we reflect on how the imprint on the Shroud is due essentially to the close adhesion of the material to every part of the body of Jesus, we must be especially grateful to the Person who, during those dramatic moments of Friday evening, took such loving care.

The Shroud was, in fact, very carefully wrapped, especially around the wounds, the swellings, the trickles of blood of that tortured body. And at the end it was tucked in in the very same way that every mother tucks in the sheets of her child in bed.

Indeed, as every mother does...

Even though we cannot show it, we can believe that in the Tomb, in the final tangible sign of maternal love to Jesus, his mother, Mary, was present.

She, who in the wonder of the whole created world, so many years earlier, had given her unconditional assent: *"Behold the handmaid of the Lord: be it unto me according to thy word"* (Luke 1: 38).

By giving birth to her Creator, the promises made to the Fathers were realised, and the History of Salvation began to flower. The God-bearer, as the Orthodox Church venerates her; the co-Redemptress, the Mother of God and the Queen of the Church. And yet, in human terms a mother, in the tender care of Bethlehem, in the anxiety in the Temple, in the daily trust in Nazareth, in the absolute faith shown in the marriage at Cana, right up to the searing pain of Calvary.

She and only she, aware of the work of Redemption: *"suffers profoundly with her first-born son, and associating herself in her maternal spirit with his sacrifice, lovingly conscious of the offering up of the victim to whom she had given birth"* (Lumen Gentium, 58).

So while the trumpets of the Temple are about to announce the opening of the Sabbath, with the consequent closing of the doors of Jerusalem, Mary, with motherly determination, sees to the burial of her son in the best possible way.

And yet, I am sure that as she entered the city together with St John, in Mary's heart sentiments of faithful awaiting and hope were still beating.

A gift of Providence, a message of hope

There is undoubtedly something to reflect on if we think how the Holy Shroud, unharmed, has come down to us, passing through twenty centuries of history.

Two thousand years marked by war, fire, invasion and pillage - to say nothing of mould, grubs and rodents - which could easily have destroyed what in terms of substance is purely a piece of linen material. But instead, the Holy Shroud is still there, silent and solemn, to remind us in these times when consumerism and materialism seem to have taken pride of place in the scale of values, of the Incarnation of the Word of God and the redemption which He wrought.

Even when subjected to the most sophisticated research and analysis, the Holy Shroud shows, to those who seek rational and demonstrable proofs today, its possible origin in the first Good Friday of history.

In all of this, excluding any extraneous miracle, we cannot deny the providential hand of the Lord. Divine Providence, wishing to give us a testimony written in blood of the Passion of Jesus, has made use of people, places and events which have guaranteed its integrity right down to our own times, now that we are capable of reading it in its entirety.

I would like to conclude with a grateful acknowledgment to Humbert II of Savoy, a man of profound faith. After nearly forty years of exile, when he was approaching his entry to that Kingdom which knows no end, and where the vision of Christ the Redeemer is eternal, he wished to ensure that at his death, the Holy Shroud, defended and venerated for centuries by his ancestors among the white mountains of the Alps, should be donated to the Supreme Pontiff.

At the threshold of the third millennium, when humanity is looking towards a future heavy with the unknown, the Holy Shroud returns as on that first Sunday of Christianity, under the eyes and the hands of Peter, "*as a unique and truly providential sign*" (John Paul II) to bring to the world His message of Faith and Hope.

"The Word was made flesh and dwelt among us... God so loved the world that He gave his only-begotten son that all who believe in him should not perish but have everlasting life".

IMAGES

From the work of Mons. Giulio Ricci

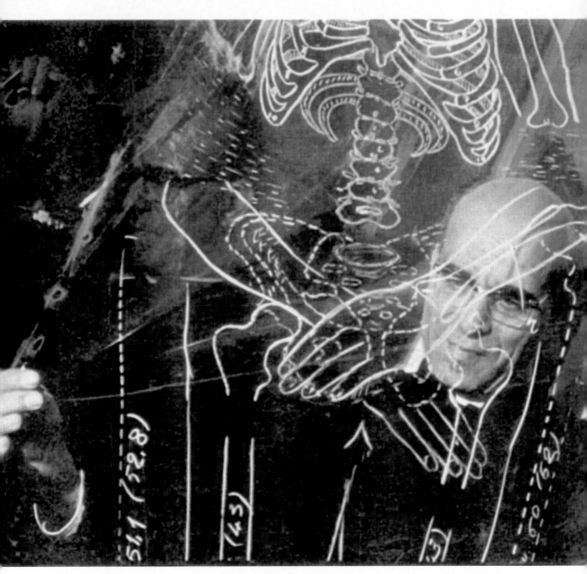

1. *Monsignor Giulio Ricci*

*2. The Holy Shroud: engraving in gold and silver, 29 x 41 cm.
(B. Robazza, G. Ricci, 1971)*

3. Reconstruction of the flagellation (1971)

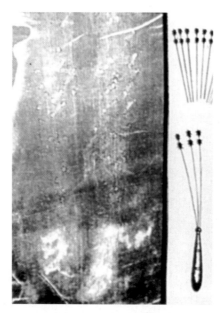

4. *Study of the flagellation on the side of the tibiae,
and reconstruction of the Flagrum taxillatum*

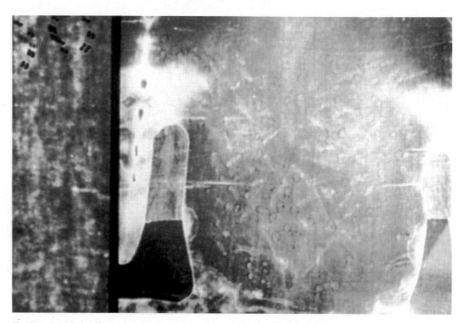

5. *Study of the flagellation in the area of the back, and detail of one of the blows*

*6. Reconstruction of the imprint of the flagellation on the back,
following the play of the rivulets of blood,
according to the evidence provided by the Shroud (G. Ricci)*

7. *The front imprint of the flagellation (G. Ricci)*

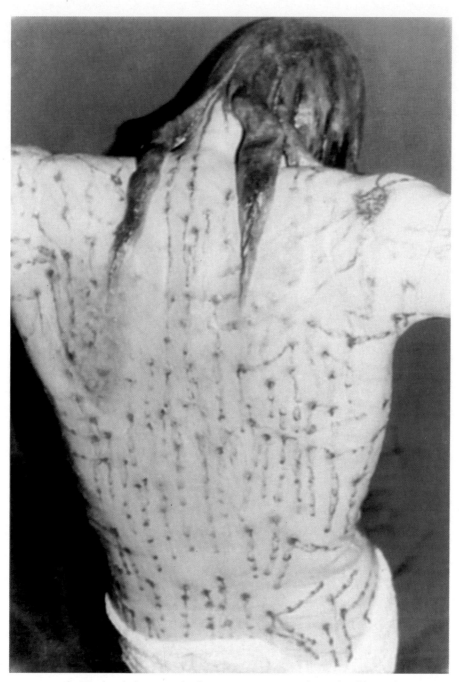

8. *Back of the crucified man as imprinted on the Shroud*

9. Jesus is condemned to death (1973)

10. *Jesus crowned with thorns (1968)*

11. *Jesus is burdened with the patibulum*

12. *Jesus falls for the first time*

13. *Reconstruction and study of the binding on the leg of the Man of the Shroud*

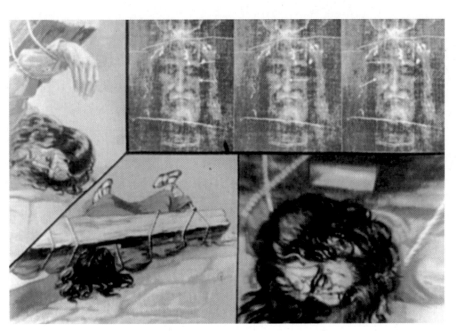

14. *Reconstruction of the falls on the Via Crucis*

15. *Jesus meets his mother*

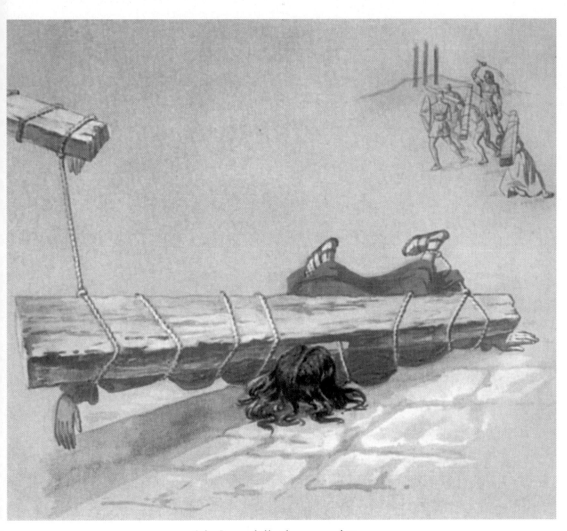

16. *Jesus falls the second time*

17. *Jesus falls the third time*

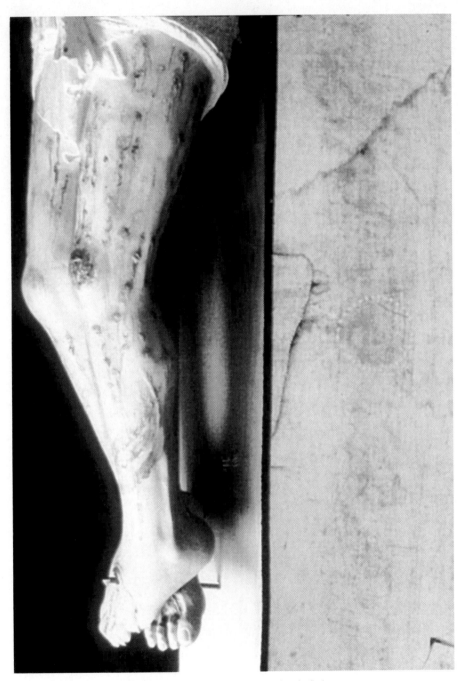

18. *Study of the injury to the left knee*

19. Simon of Cyrene carries the cross

20. Jesus comforts the women of Jerusalem

21. Jesus is stripped of his garments

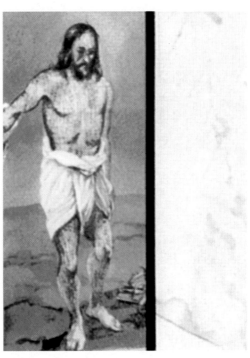

22. Study of the stripping of the garments

23. *The Veil of Veronica*

24. *Jesus is nailed to the Cross*

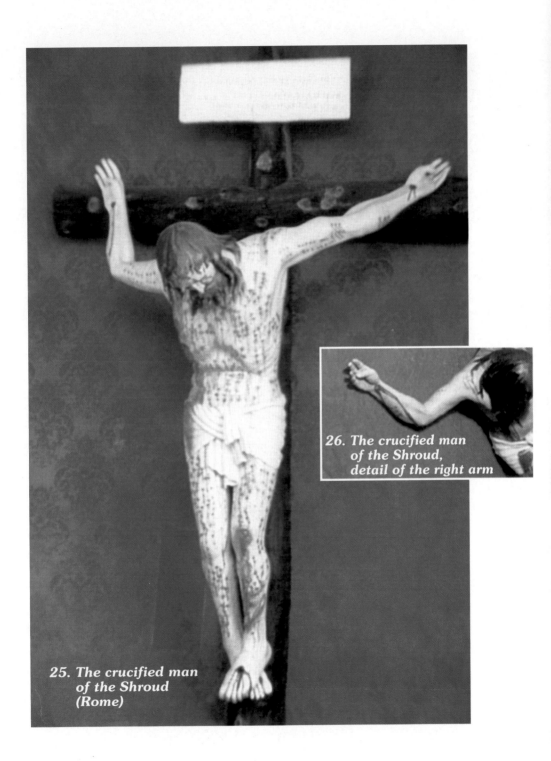

25. The crucified man
of the Shroud
(Rome)

26. The crucified man
of the Shroud,
detail of the right arm

27. Detail of the crucified man of the Shroud

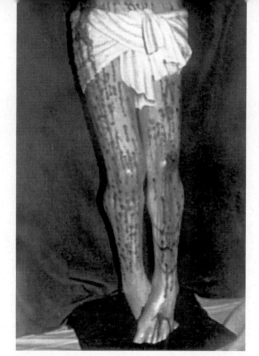

28. Crucified man of the Shroud: detail of the legs

29. Jesus dies on the Cross

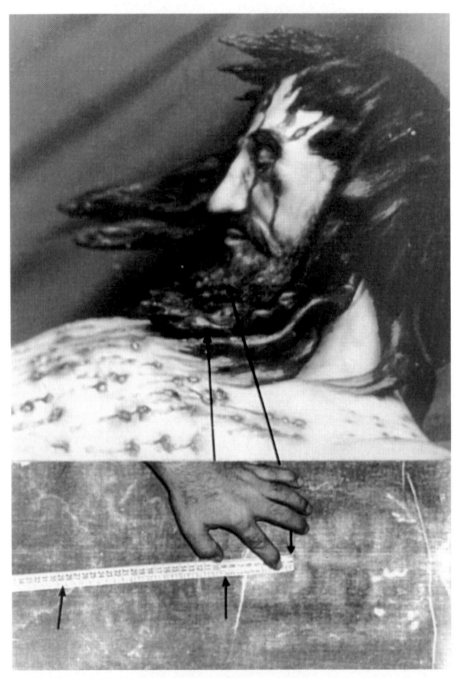

30. *Study of the bowed head*

31. *Jesus is taken down from the Cross*

32. *Jesus is wrapped in the Shroud*

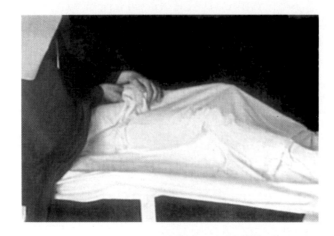

33. *Tucking-in of the sheet under the right hand*

34. *Tucking-in of the sheet around the forearm*

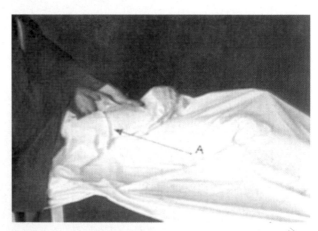

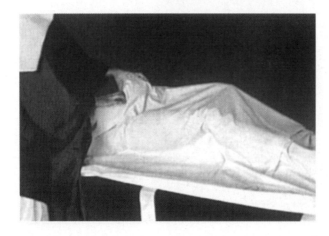

35. *Tucking-in of the sheet above the right wrist*

36. *Tucking-in of the sheet at the right femur*

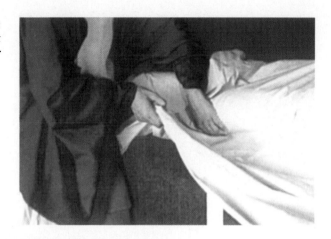

37. *Tucking-in of the sheet at the feet*

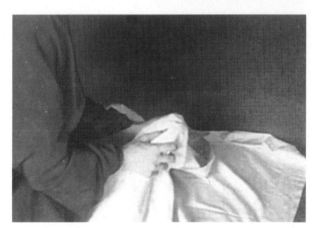

38. *Folding over of the Shroud at the tibiae*

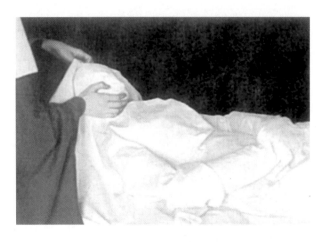

39. *Tucking-in
of the sheet
around the face*

40. *Binding
with strips
of cloth*

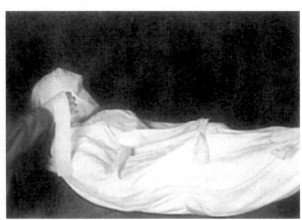

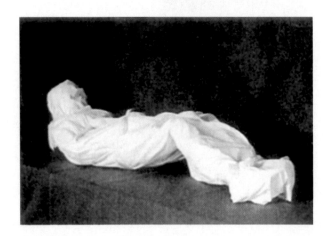

41. *Reconstruction
of the wrapping
of the Shroud
around the body*

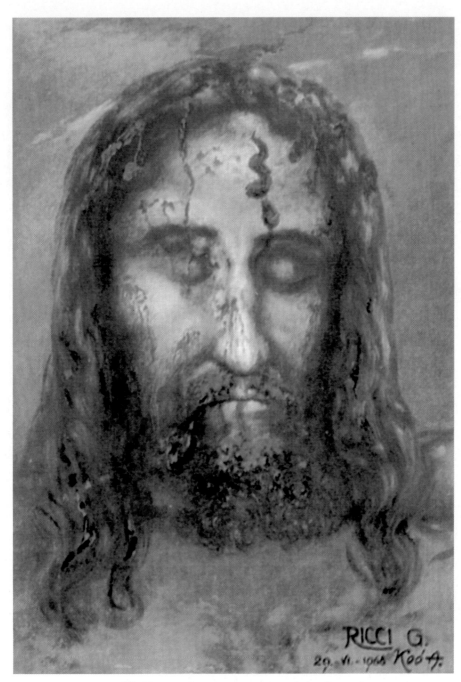

42. Pictorial reconstruction of the face

43. *Jesus rises again*

44. *The Holy Shroud in a painting of the 17ᵗʰ century
(painted on material – Ricci collection)*

45. *Reconstruction of the Basilica of the Holy Sepulchre,
and ampulla of Monza*

46. *Electronic reconstruction of the face on the shroud (A. Cacciani)*

47. The Napkin of Oviedo-Luce, by Wood U.V.
Parallel comparison with the miscroscopic imprints of the blood (photo Salazzi)

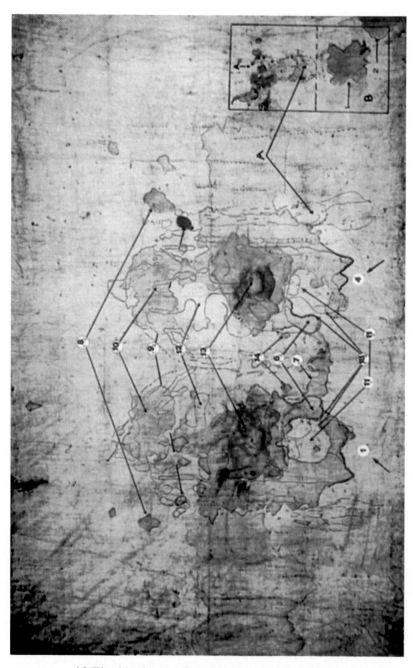

48 The Napkin of Oviedo-Luce, by Wood U.V.
Parallel comparisons with the linear traces of the face on the Shroud

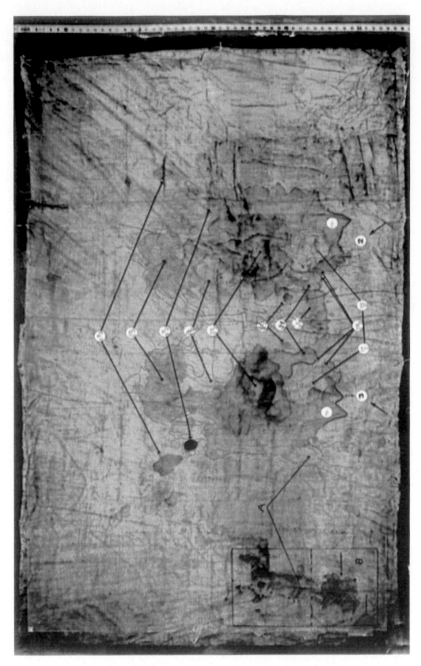

49. The Napkin of Oviedo-Luce, by Wood U.V.
Parallel comparison with the reverse side

50. Image of the Sacred Visage superimposed on the Oviedo Napkin

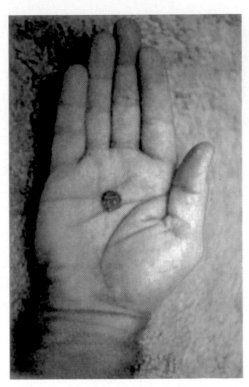

51. Proportion
    of the Lepton
    with the palm
    of the hand

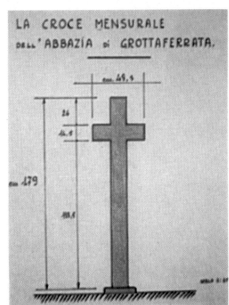

52. Mensural Cross
of the Abbey of Grottaferrata
(P. Solaini)

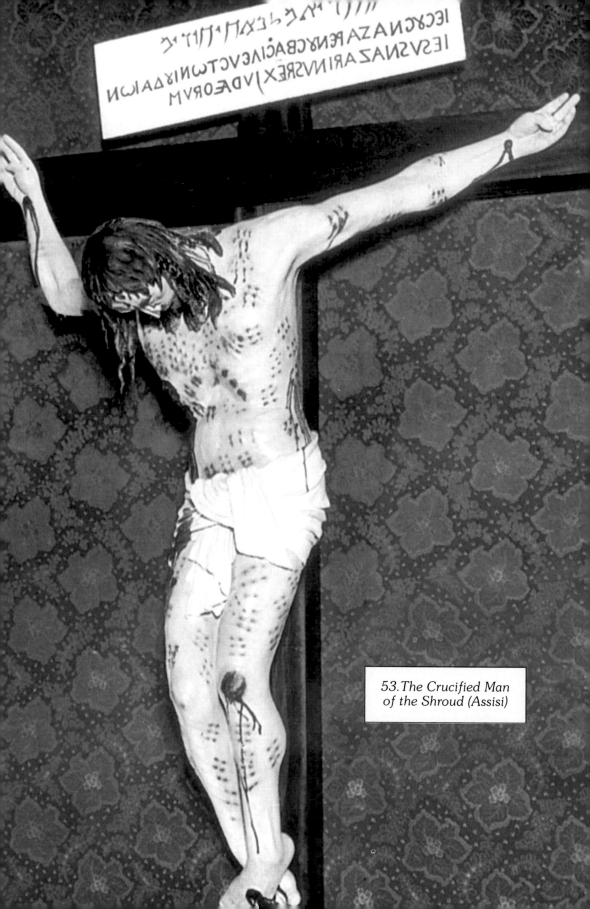

53. The Crucified Man
of the Shroud (Assisi)

Prayer before the Shroud

Imprint Your face on mine, O Lord,
So that the Father may see You in me,
And repeat "You are my beloved son".
And so that all who meet with me
May see a spark of the Father's presence.

Imprint your face on mine, O Lord,
So that I may be a witness
of Your light and your goodness;
and of the infinite tenderness
which You have for every creature

Imprint your face on mine, O Lord,
So that I may be a sign of Your love
For the small and the poor,
For the sick and the alienated

Imprint Your face on mine, O Lord
so that I may be a living Shroud
which bears in itself the signs
of Your death and resurrection.

Anon.

THE SHROUD AND THE HOUSE OF SAVOY

The desire to ensure a secure future for the family fortunes, the need to find protection in those difficult times, the wish to intercede on behalf of an adopted nephew who had fallen into disgrace, all led Margherita di Charny, the last descendent of her house, to entrust the Shroud to the possession of Duke Louis of Savoy.

Thus began an intense and fascinating story, which would link the fate of the Shroud to that of the House of Savoy throughout five centuries of rich cultural artistic and religious events, but also of war, aggression and invasion.

This story has as its protagonists a thousand year old dynasty, involving thirteen Dukes of Savoy, seven Kings of Sardinia and four Kings of Italy, in defending and preserving this, one of the most important relics of Christendom, and increasing knowledge and veneration of it, and devotion to it.

The House of Savoy, coming from a small region hidden away among the white mountains of the western Alps between France and Switzerland, finds its earliest documented origins in the mythical figure of Umberto di Biancamano, considered the founder of the dynasty.

Created Counts of Moriana a little after the year 1000, they became Dukes of Savoy in 1416, Kings of Sicily from 1713 to 1719, Kings of Sardinia in 1720, and by crowning the Risorgimento's dream of the freedom and unity of the whole peninsula, Kings of Italy from 1861.

The presence of the Shroud in the territory of Savoy, and especially in Turin, has played a determining role both in the religious sense and in political terms. The Holy Shroud was in fact to represent the symbol of the Savoy Dynasty and its subjects for 500 years. A sure sign of heavenly blessing and protection in daily life and in adversity: a reference point for faith.

Among many other episodes, a particularly significant one is the Battle of Lepanto (7 October 1571), when the Admiral of the

Savoy fleet, which was taking part in the 'Holy League' with three ships, on the orders of Duke Emanuel Philibert raised not the official flag but one on which the holy shroud was portrayed.

From the political viewpoint, moreover, the Shroud was to be the sign of legitimisation of the reigning house, the expression of divine preference which gave the House of Savoy privileges over other dynasties to safeguard the Shroud of Christ.

And the Savoys, aware of this role, lived it with faith, confirming it from one generation to another in their constancy to the commitment undertaken by their ancestors, and with sovereign greatness.

Witness the building of the Sainte Chapelle at Chambéry (Amadeus IX), the minting of coinage (Louis I, Charles I, Emanuel Philibert), the institution of the liturgical feast of the Shroud and the Holy Eucharist on 4 May (Charles III and Pope Julius II), the building of the baroque gem represented by the Chapel of the Shroud in Turin, with the world-famous dome by Guarini, as well as constant and repeated rescue during enemy incursion, until the generous decision of the last King of Italy, Humbert II was reached, inspired by Christian devotion, to donate the Shroud to the Pope.

This link between the Shroud and the Savoys which began (according to tradition) on 22 March 1453, was to become more and more profound in the course of the centuries, producing a deep and rooted devotion to the Passion of Christ among the faithful. There are eloquent testimonies of this, especially in Piedmont, such as the votive chapels and the institutes of Charity, the social and charitable works which have arisen and developed in the name of the Holy Shroud.

Of key importance was the spiritual support of the three Savoys declared Blessed – Amadeus, Ludovica and Margherita, of the Venerable Maria Clothilde, and of certain figures of outstanding moral stature, devoted to the Shroud and close to the Savoy family: St Charles Borromeo, St Francis de Sales and the Blessed Sebastian Valfré.

A particular place in the relationship between the Shroud, the Savoys and the Faithful, has been held by the public displays of the relic. These, linked to historical and dynastic events in the House of Savoy, were traditionally allowed on the occasion of marriages, baptisms or other special circumstances. They were prepared and took place by way of a solemn ceremony, which provided for the sovereigns to take part, along with the Court and the highest civil and religious authorities, and they created an extraordinary involvement among all the people who came, as they still do today, to venerate the holy relic in Turin.

An invaluable record in images of these events is provided by the collection of prints gathered with devotion and skill by Humbert II, and now held by the Humbert II and Maria José of Savoy Foundation.

We can therefore state that the Shroud and the Savoys are an "indissoluble partnership", as the Archbishop of Turin, Mgr. Severino Poletto recently called it, and this partnership, far from being split up by the donation to the Church, has been finally confirmed by it.

Donation of His Majesty King Umberto II of Savoy,
Last King of Italy, to the Holy See
(Entrusting his Will to his nephews)

To His Majesty Simeon of Bulgaria
To His Royal Highness Maurice of Hesse

In consideration of the veneration which the Catholic Church dedicates to the Holy Shroud, conserved in the Chapel of the Cathedral of Turin,

Having confirmed that the Catholic Hierarchy acknowledges that the House of Savoy, in the embodiment of its Head, owns historical rights of property on the Holy Shroud.

I feel it just to entrust the Catholic Church with one of the most outstanding Relics demonstrating the Passion of Our Lord,

I DECREE THAT

after my death, the entire property of the Holy Shroud shall be donated to the Holy See.

Donated together with the Holy Shroud, should also be all that which pertains to the same, conserved within the Chapel of the Cathedral of Turin, being as such an extension of my personal belongings.

I ask that you, my testimonial executors, effectuate all those issues necessary to the notification of these, my wishes, to the Pontiff, until such that He can appropriate the responsibility for the Holy Shroud.

It is my desire that, as a seal of this consignment of such property, an official document be scripted together with the Holy See, which in view of this, my present situation, I delegate you my executors, to precede towards its finalisation and signature.

Geneva, 27th March 1981   *Umberto*

"GIULIO RICCI"
DIOCESAN CENTRE FOR STUDY
OF THE HOLY SHROUD

The "Giulio Ricci" Diocesan Centre for Study of the Holy Shroud (Sindonology), instituted on 2 January 1986 by His Eminence Cardinal Camillo Ruini, Vicar-General of His Holiness for the Diocese of Rome, to promote the study and knowledge of the Holy Shroud of Turin, is dedicated to Monsignor Giulio Ricci, a priest of the Roman Church, who throughout his life was the leading devotee of the Shroud, a researcher of strict comparative scientific method and the guiding spirit of a devotional cult based on sound convictions of the purest faith.

The Centre, which has its offices at the Basilica of Santa Croce in Gerusalemme, has the aim of promoting and augmenting the study of the sacred cloth image of the Passion, a special instrument for spiritual and ecclesiastical training in the proclamation of Easter.

The Centre pursues its own aims by training persons who are prepared in the spreading of the Gospel message, by means of a special knowledge of the mystery of the Passion and Resurrection of the Lord Jesus, through:
- courses of further training in the scientific, historical and theological disciplines which deal with the Shroud;
- lectures;
- conferences;
- exhibitions;
- spiritual encounters.

In particular, in collaboration with the Vicariate of Rome, the Centre has promoted and coordinated the Course in Sindonology at the "Ecclesia Mater" Institute of the Pontifical University of the Lateran. The course, divided into "The Gospel and the Shroud" and "The Shroud and Science" made use of the teaching services of scholarly teachers from the Pontifical and State Universities.

The Centre has also edited the publication "La Sindone sulle orme di Monsignor Giulio Ricci" (The Shroud in the Footsteps of Monsignor Giulio Ricci), a special number of the Diocesan Review of Rome, and it provided a consultancy to the Vatican Philatelic Office for the issue of a stamp dedicated to the Shroud, on the occasion of its public display in 1998.

SANTA CROCE IN HISTORY AND FAITH

"Here we are in the true sanctuary of the Cross!" With these words, the Holy Father John Paul II greeted Santa Croce in Gerusalemme during his pastoral visit on 25 March 1979. The title is more than justified for this ancient Basilica, with its close links to the Passion of Christ.

Among the places of worship built during the era of Constantine, Santa Croce was intended and designed to be a Sanctuary, similar to those built in the Holy Land over the sites that had witnessed the Death and Resurrection of Jesus. In contrast to these, however, the object of veneration here was not associated with the place, but had been transferred there.

Known as the Basilica Heleniana or Sessoriana, the fourth century church was made out of a great hall of the Sessorium, the Imperial Palace on the slopes of the Esquiline Hill, where Helena the mother of the Emperor Constantine lived. It was intended to receive and guard the relics of the Passion which had been brought to light in the Holy Land itself.

In the course of its sixteen centuries of history, the Basilica has been constantly renewed in form, and has been enriched with works of art and culture; above all, however, it has left a profound mark on the spiritual life of Rome and the Universal Church.

Rites and traditions linked to the cult of the Cross have been characteristic of its history since its origins. A part of the "stational" pilgrimage journey through Rome, Santa Croce is a "statio" on two occasions in Lent, the fourth Sunday and Good Friday. Solemn liturgies are also celebrated on the Feast of the Exaltation of the Cross on 14 September, and the Invention (i.e. Finding) of the Cross on 3 May.

Since the mid-sixteenth century, the Basilica has been on the route of the Seven Churches which was organised by St Philip Neri; it was a Jubilee Basilica on the occasion of the special Holy Years of the Redemption, and it still played this role, at the behest of John Paul II, on the occasion of the Great Jubilee of the Year 2000.

THE SESSORIAN RELICS

It is a tradition of great antiquity that a part of the Cross of Our Lord was brought to Rome and venerated in the Sessorian Basilica.

Sources from late antiquity and the mediaeval period bear witness to this, and confirm the ancient rituals of the Papal ceremonies, which established the Adoration of the Cross on Good Friday in Hierusalem: the Pope in person walked barefoot from the Lateran Basilica and went in procession with the clergy and people to the Sessorian Basilica to venerate the wood of the true Holy Cross. Over the centuries a number of fragments of the Sacred Wood were taken from the Sessorian Reliquary to be given by the Popes to individuals and Churches: Gregory the Great sent a fragment as a gift to Reccaredo King of the Visgoths; Leo X had part of it extracted to present to Francis I, King of France (1515); Urban VIII (1623-1644) decided to give part to the Vatican Basilica, and Pius VI, Pius VII and Pius IX all had small fragments of it removed.

Even though it is such an ancient relic, therefore, it can adduce numerous documents which attest its discovery, transfer, preservation and veneration.

With regard to the Nail, too, the tradition is ancient and constant; in fact the finding of the nails with which Jesus was crucified is also attributed to St Helena. The Empress had one inserted into the crown of Constantine and one into the bridle of his horse. She brought another with her to Rome, and this is probably the one of which Gregory of Tours speaks: St Helena, during her return from Palestine, found the sea very rough, and had one of the nails from the Crucifixion plunged into the water: immediately on contact, the sea was calmed. It was always included among the Sessorian relics, and together with that of Milan, is one of the most ancient to be documented.

As far as the relic of the Inscription is concerned – the wooden board with part of the inscription Jesus Nazarenus Rex Iudaeorum in Hebrew, Greek and Latin – tradition gives way to history at a certain point. Stefano Infessura, in his Diary, on 1 February 1492, recounts that this relic was found by chance during the work of restoration in the Basilica ordered by Cardinal Mendoza. Enclosed in a relic case with the seal of Cardinal Caccianemici, the titular of Santa Croce, and later Pope under the title of Lucius II (1144-45) – it had been walled up *ab antiquo* in the arch which separates the transept from the central nave. In ancient times relics were very often placed high up in the churches to preserve them from theft, but in the case of the Inscription, it seems that the memory of its presence was lost, because the mosaic letters which indicated its position had collapsed. The news of its rediscovery created a great sensation in that epoch, partly because it coincided with the Spanish reconquest of Granada, the last stronghold of the Arabs in the west. Pope Alexander VI Borgia issued the bull *Admirabile sacramentum* on 29 July 1496, by which he authenticated the rediscovery of the Inscription and granted plenary indulgence to those who visited Santa Croce on the last Sunday in January.

Tradition does not, on the other hand, attribute the discovery of the Crown of Thorns to St Helena. We know that this relic was already venerated in Constantinople in the time of Justinian. During the time of the Latin Kingdom in the East (1204-1261), the Venetians had it in their possession. In 1270, it was taken by St Louis, King of France, who placed it in the Chapel of the Royal

Palace. Subsequently it passed to the Abbey of St Denis (1791) and finally in 1806 was transferred to Notre Dame, where it is still preserved. It is devoid of thorns, which are scattered among many churches.

Other relics have been added over the ages to the relics of the Passion of Christ – such as fragments of the cave of Bethlehem and of the Holy Sepulchre, and the pillar of the Flagellation; the patibulum of the Virtuous Thief, and the phalanx of the finger of St Thomas – to complete the Catechesis on the Passion. For the Church and for the pilgrims of yesterday and today, in fact, the Relics are valuable teaching instruments, signs of a certain fact, the veneration of which can assist meditation on the sufferings which they recall, and remind us of the saving power of the Cross.

IMAGES

From the work of Mons. Giulio Ricci

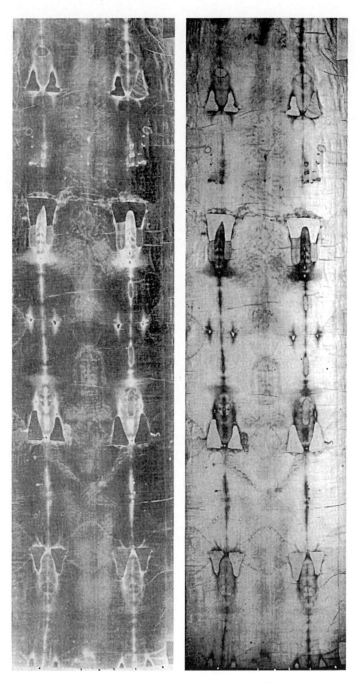

1. Holy Shroud (G. Enrie 1931)

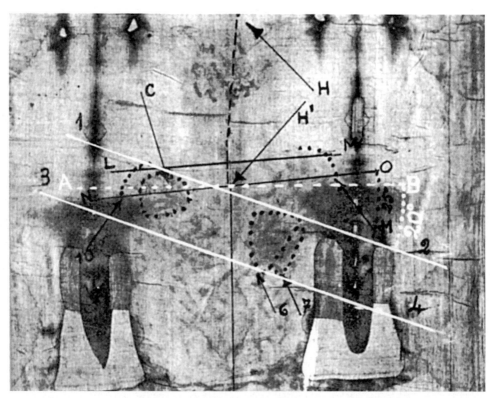

2. Study of the contusions of the scapula zone

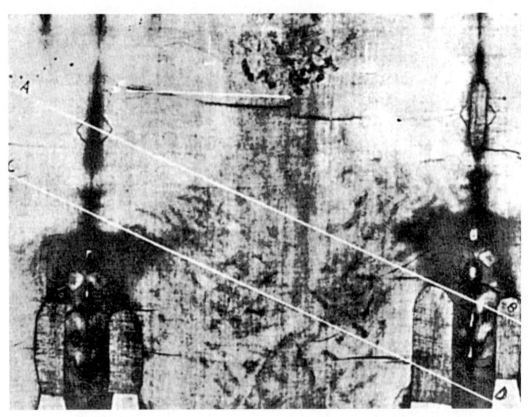

3. *Study of the oblique direction of the patibulum on the scapula zone*

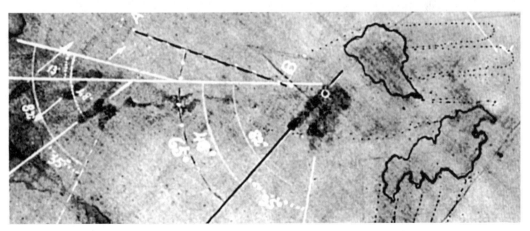

4. *Study of the kinetics of the blood trickles of the right arm*

5. Study for a Pietà

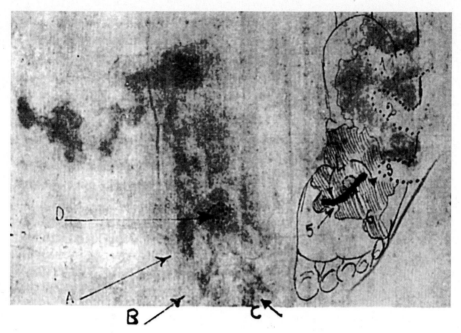

6. *Study of the side imprint of the feet*

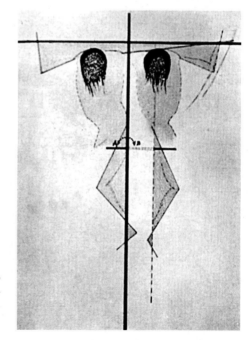

7. *Graphic study
of a crucifix
with support
at the perineum*

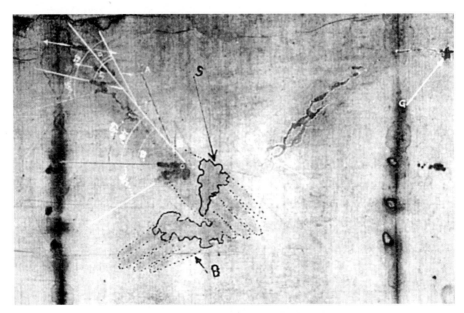

8. Study of the contusions in the metacarpal zone

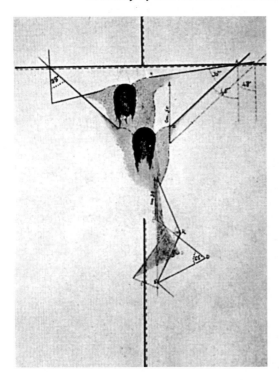

*9. Assynometry
of the movements
on the cross*

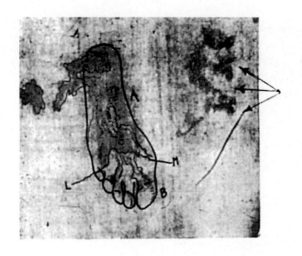

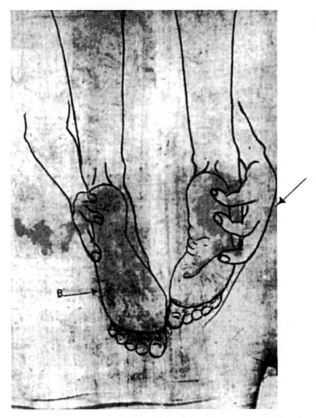

10. *Study of the kinetics of the blood in the zone of the feet*

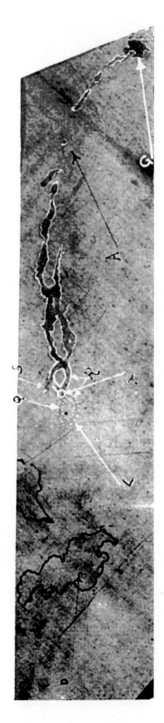

11. *Interruption of the flow of*
   blood on the right forearm

12. *Study of the imprint by osmosis on the right forearm*

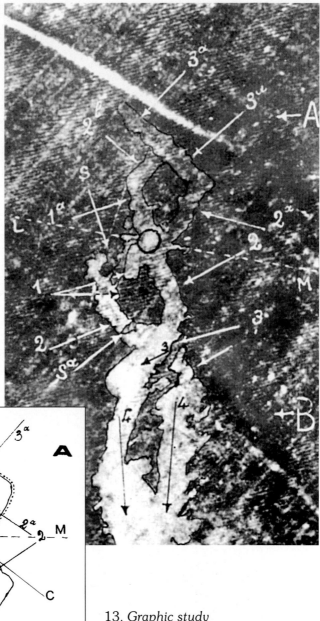

13. *Graphic study of the imprint by osmosis on the right fore-arm*

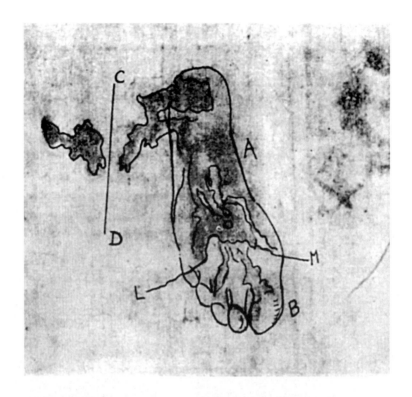

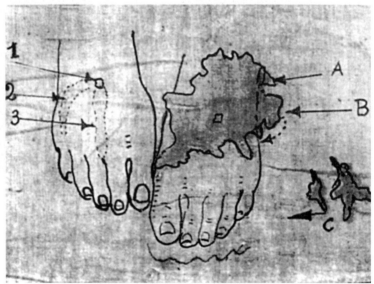

14. *Study of the blood marks on the feet*

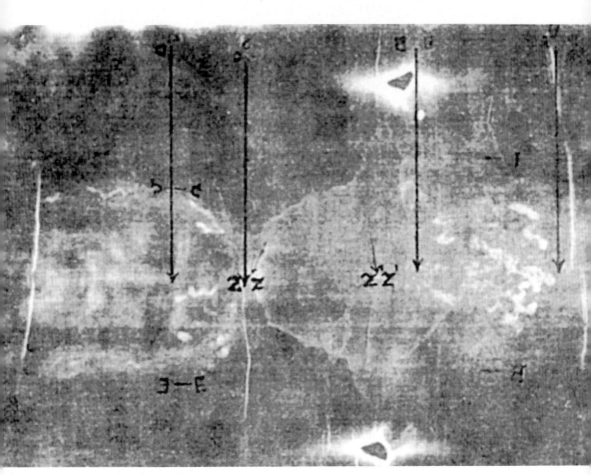

15. *Study of the epicranial space*

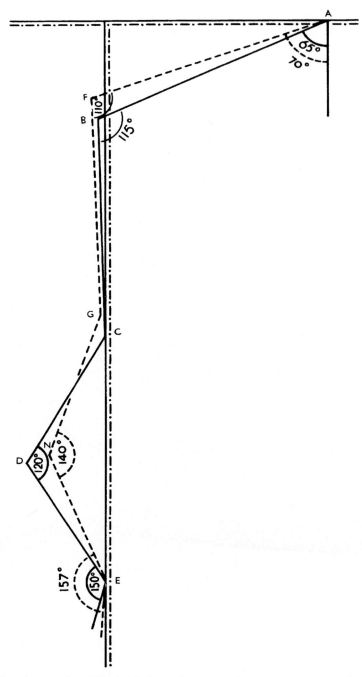

16. *Graphic study of Barbet's hypothesis on the movements on the cross*

17. *Study of the wound of the nail in the right wrist*

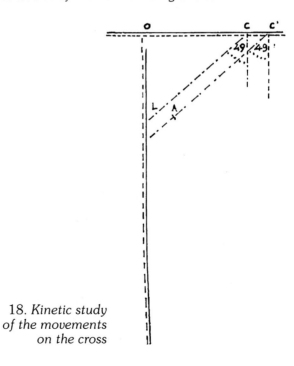

18. *Kinetic study of the movements on the cross*

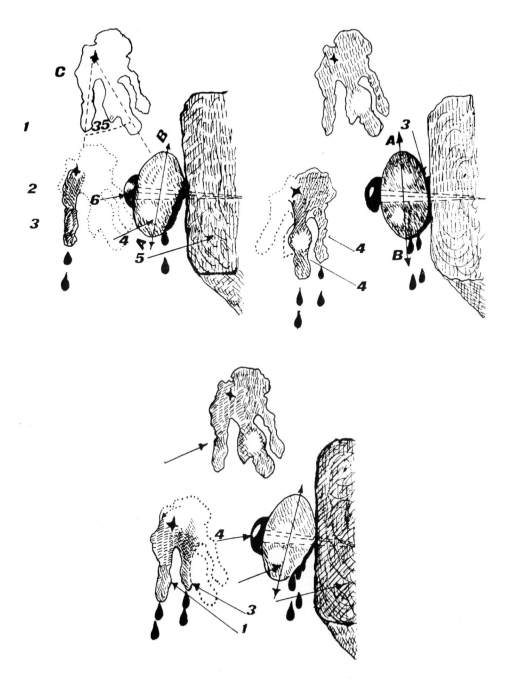

*19 - 20. Graphic study of the wound and the blood flow
of the carpus of the left hand*

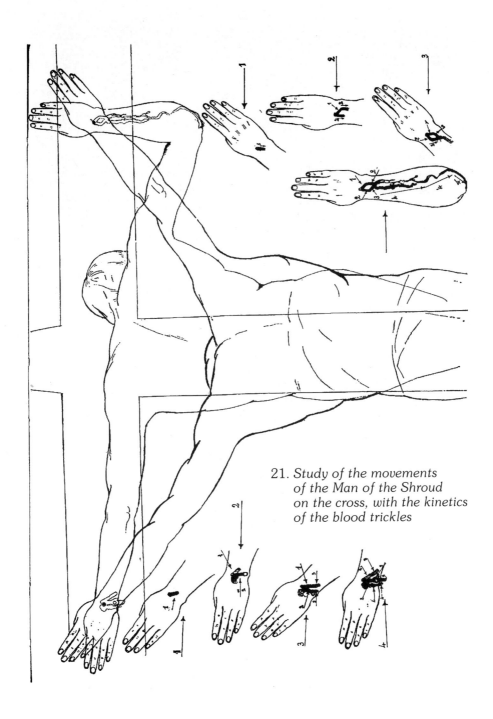

21. *Study of the movements
of the Man of the Shroud
on the cross, with the kinetics
of the blood trickles*

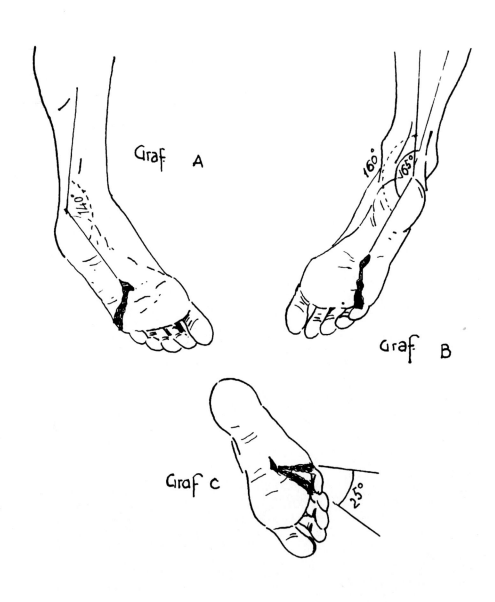

Graf A

140°

160° 165°

Graf B

Graf c

25°

22. *Study of the positions of the feet on the cross*

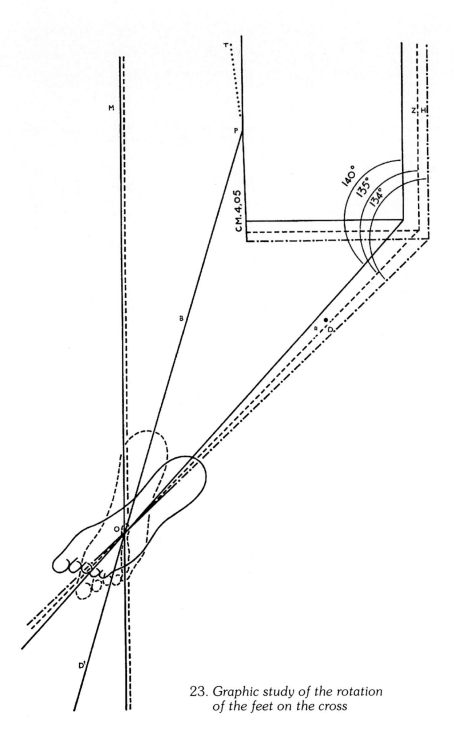

23. *Graphic study of the rotation*
of the feet on the cross

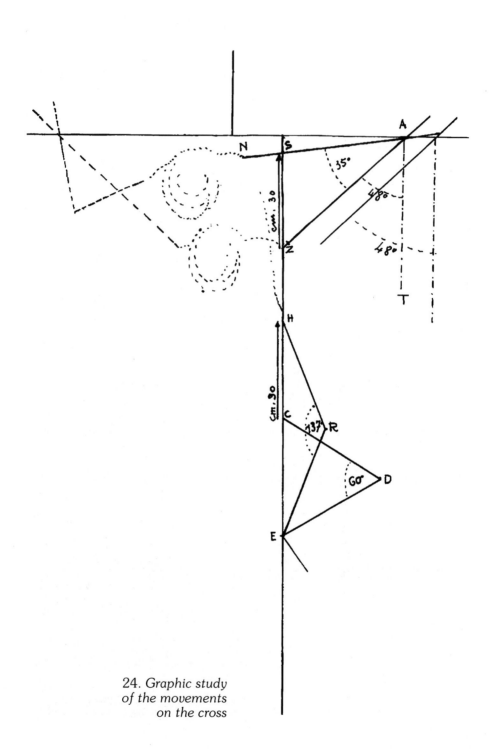

24. *Graphic study*
of the movements
on the cross

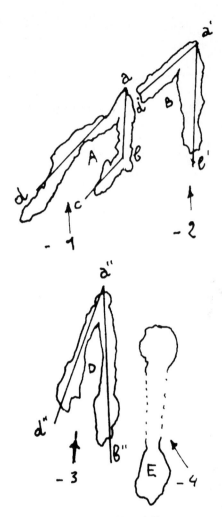

25. *Study of the blood flow from the forehead*

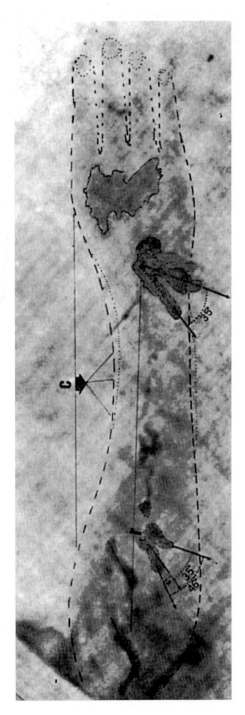

26. *Study of blood flow*

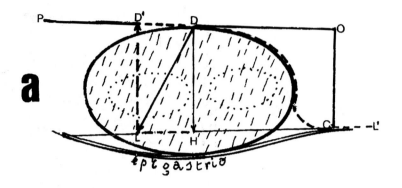

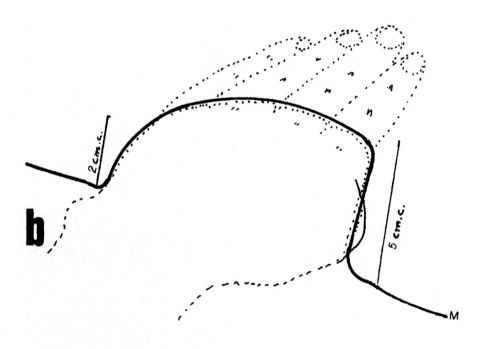

27. *Graphic study of the wrapping of the shroud around the forearms*

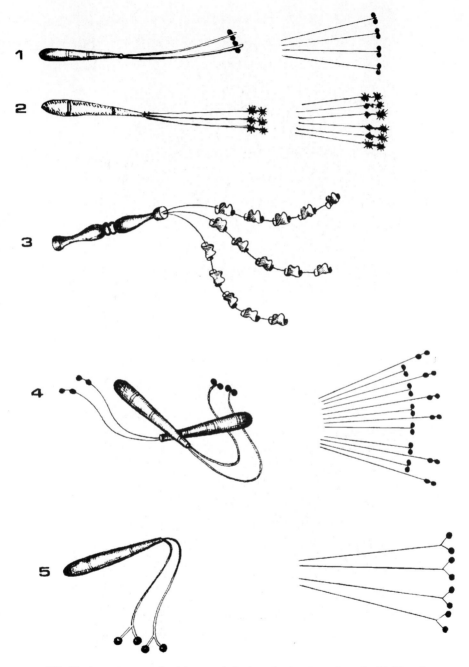

28. Various types of whips and their relative imprints (r. G. Ricci)

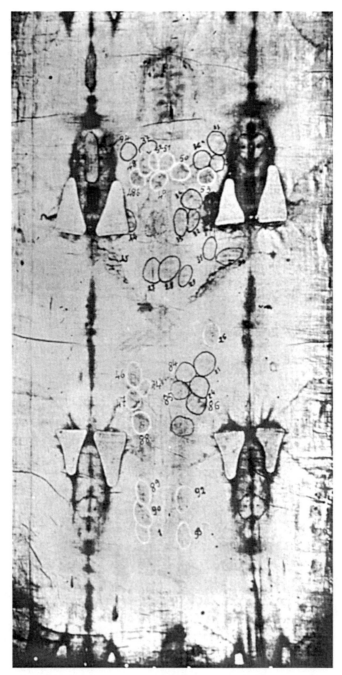

29. Study of the flagellation (front imprint)

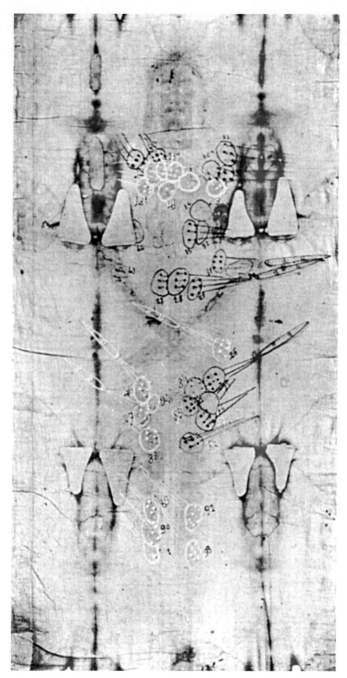

30. *Study of the flagellation (front imprint)*

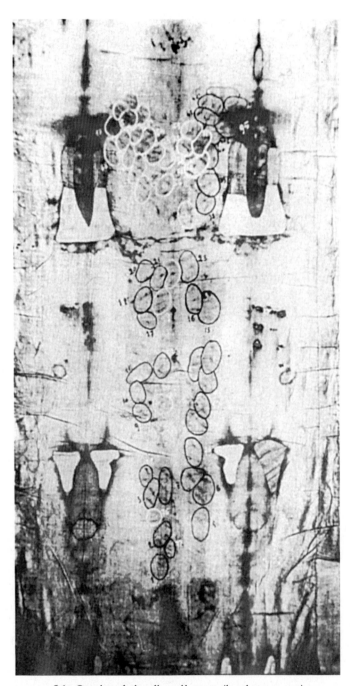

31. *Study of the flagellation (back imprint)*

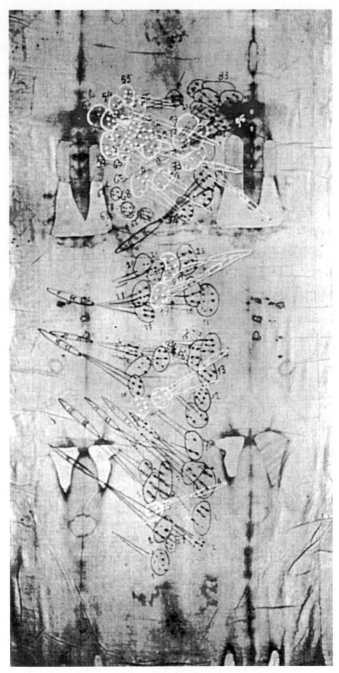

32. *Study of the flagellation (back imprint)*

33. *Drawing of
the flagellation*

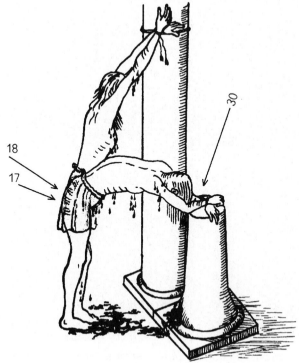

18

17

30

34. *Study of
the position
of the Man
of the Shroud
during the
flagellation*

35. *Kinetics of the blood trickles following the flagellation*

36. Reconstruction
of the Face
from the
Shroud

37. *Reconstruction of the Via Crucis*

38. Reconstruction of the falls on the Via Crucis

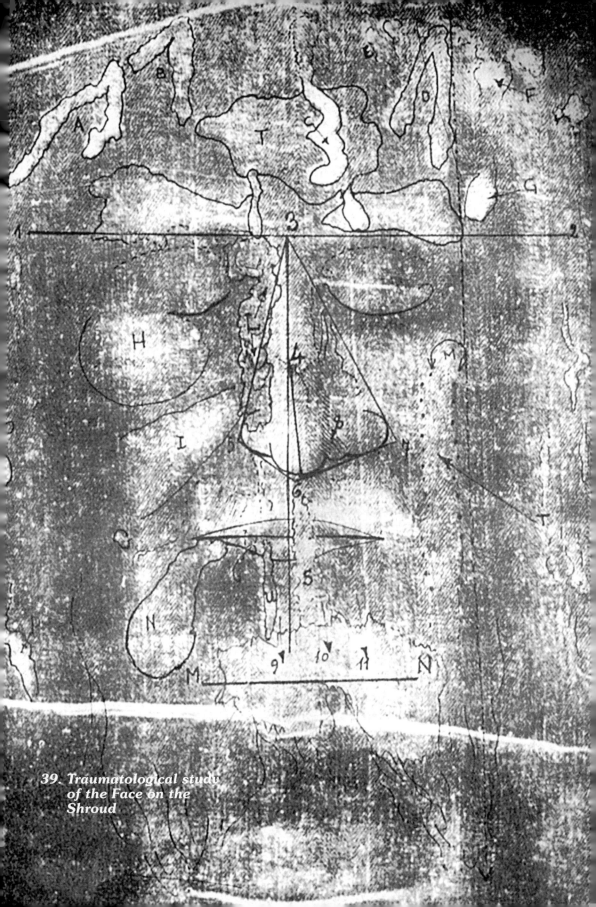

39. Traumatological study
of the Face on the
Shroud

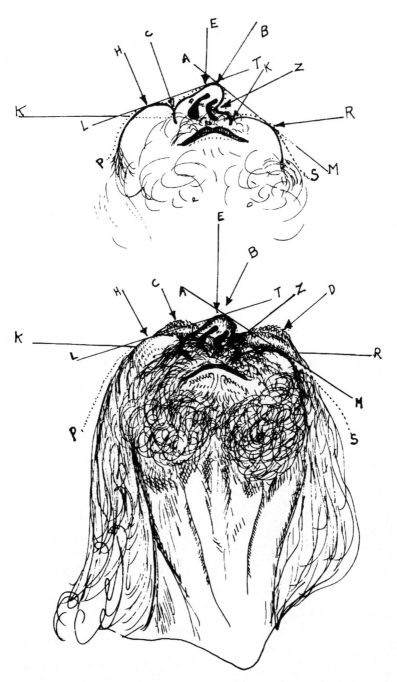

40. *Study of the wrapping of the shroud around the face*

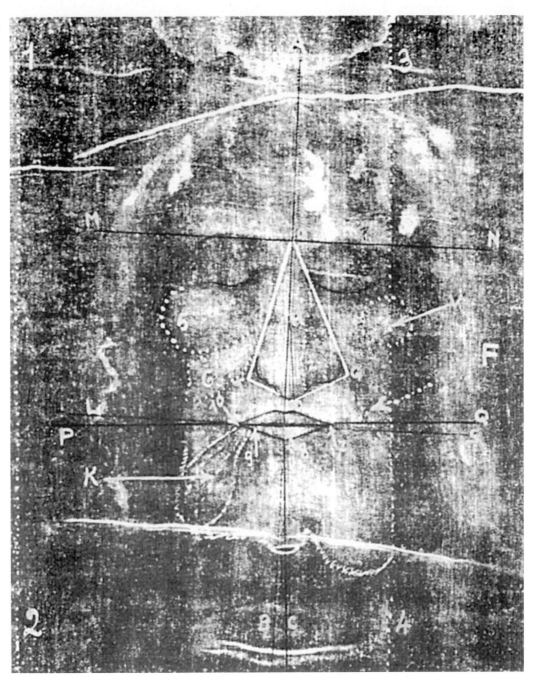

41. *Geometric study of the facial lesions*

42. Reconstruction of the left side of the face of the man on the Shroud

43. *Attempted reconstruction of the face from the Shroud*

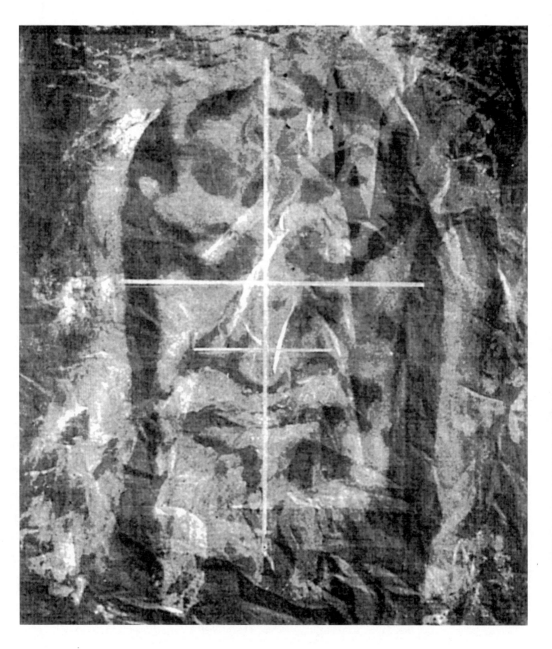

44. Negative imprint on linen of the reconstruction of the face from the Shroud

45. *Study of the Face from the Shroud over the Oviedo Napkin*

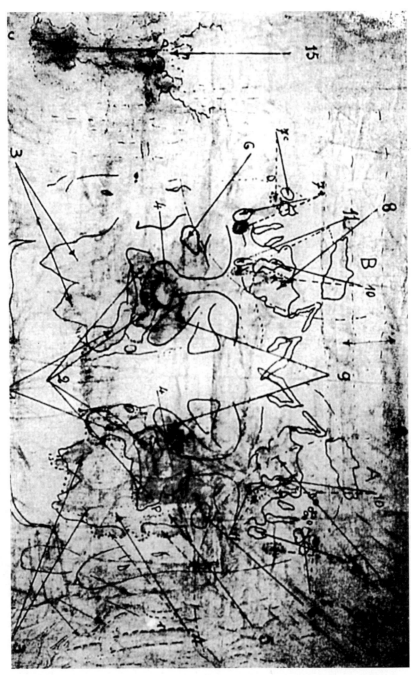

46. *Study of the Face from the Shroud over the Oviedo Napkin*

130

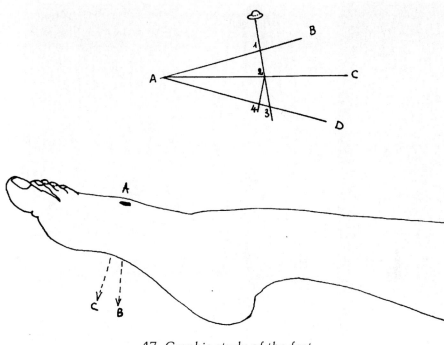

47. *Graphic study of the feet*

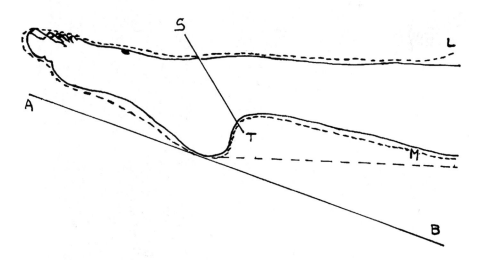

48. *Study of the wrapping of the shroud around the right foot*

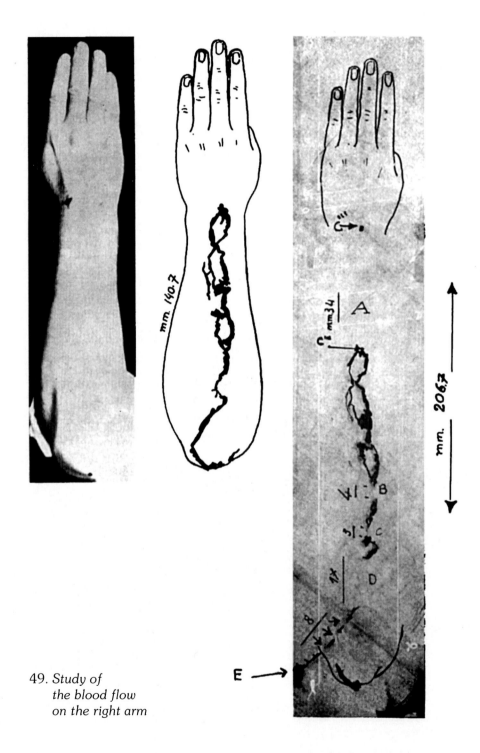

49. *Study of
the blood flow
on the right arm*

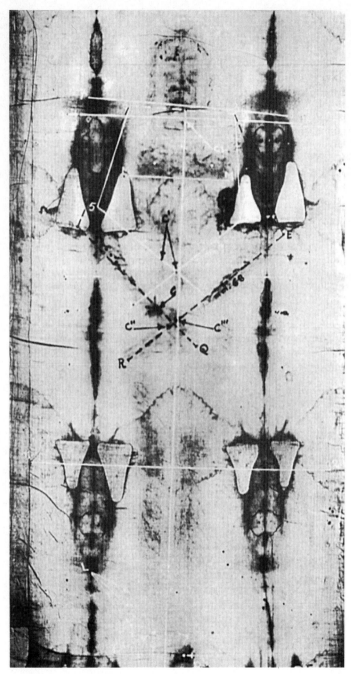

50. *Study on the anatomical asymmetry (front view)*

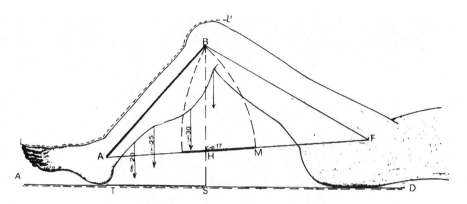

51. *Graphic study of imprint of the tibiae*

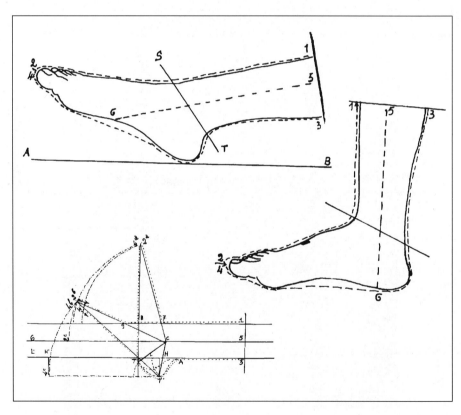

52. *Study and graphic design of the linear imprint of the feet*

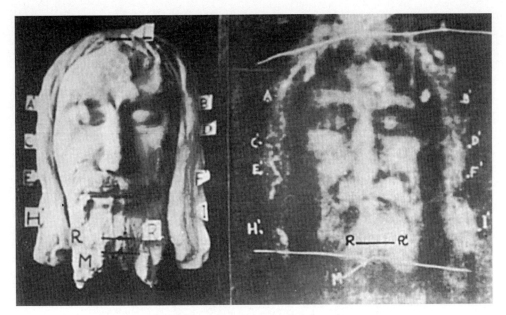

53. *Linear development of the facial imprint*

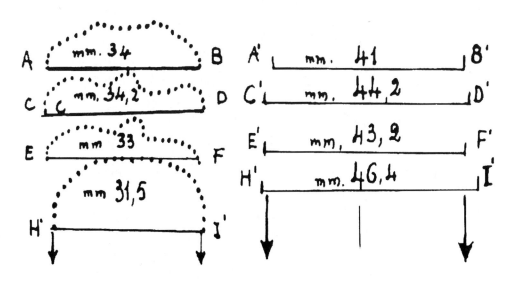

54. *Graphic design of the linear development of the facial imprint*

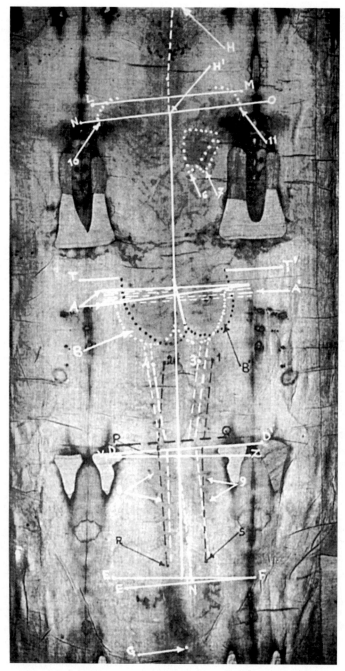

55. Study on the anatomical asymmetry (rear view)

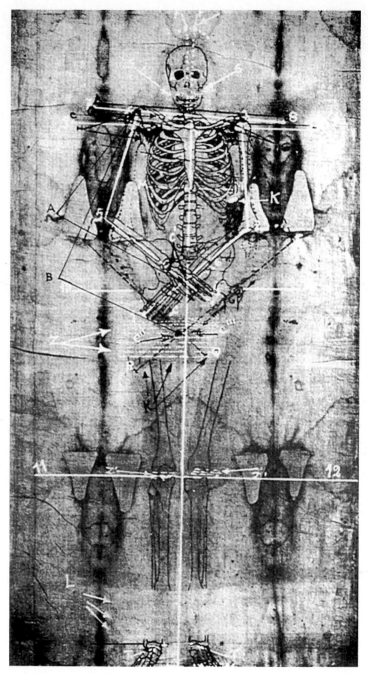

56. *Examination of the front part with skeleton superimposed*

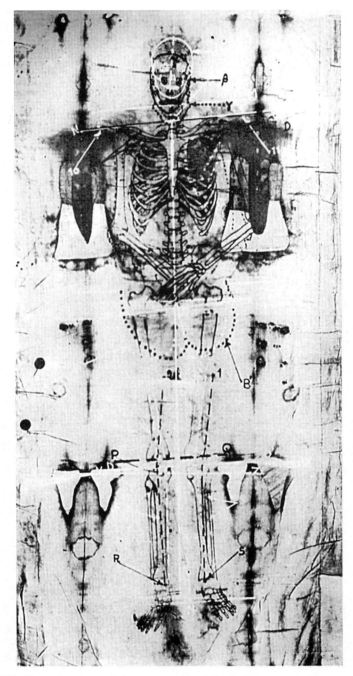

57. Examination of the rear part with skeleton superimposed

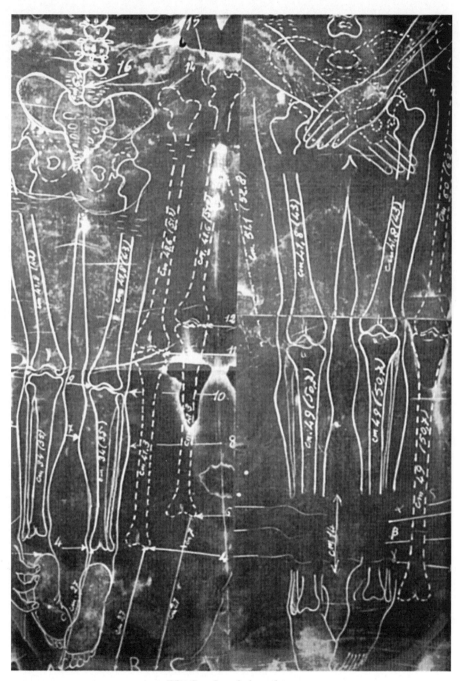

58. *Study of the tibiae*